THE · COMPLETE · GUIDE · TO

Home Video Production

A TEN-STEP PLAN FOR MAKING YOUR OWN TELEVISION PROGRAM

Pamela Levine · Jeffrey Glasser · Stephen Gach

An Owl Book
Holt, Rinehart and Winston New York

Library of Congress Cataloging in Publication Data
Levine, Pamela
The complete guide to—home video production.
Rev. ed. of: The complete guide to—home video
programming, 1983.
"An Owl book."
1. Video recordings—Production and direction—Hand-
books, manuals, etc. I. Glasser, Jeffrey. II. Gach,
Stephen. III. Levine, Pamela. The complete guide
to—home video programming. IV. Title. V. Title: Home
video production.
PN1992.95.L48   1984   791.43'0232   83-26462
ISBN 0-03-071082-0

First published by Videowares Publishing Company in 1983.
First Owl Book Edition—1984

Printed in the United States of America
1 3 5 7 9 10 8 6 4 2

ISBN 0-03-071082-0

ACKNOWLEDGMENTS

<u>Our Special Thanks for Support to</u>

G. L. Harrington, encouragement and guidance

Cheryl Brantner, design and layout

Terry Borst, editing and word processing

Steve Blackwell, editing and rewrites

Stephen Gach, photography   5005883

Marianne DiLiberto, coordination and typing

Johanna & Alexis Gach and Stefanie & Carolyn Glasser,
   love, understanding, and photographic talent

Tree Locke, photographic talent

Sony Corporation of America, equipment support

Laura Sihoven, diagrams and illustrations

DEDICATION

To our parents and families for all their love and support.

FOREWORD

Home Video Production (HVP) offers an easy 10-step approach to making your own video programs of professional quality. We have designed the book to be comprehensive, yet practical enough for the beginner. Our step-by-step method introduces specific skills and production information which will make your programs easier to produce and more enjoyable to watch. You will learn how to become a TV producer and build exciting video albums documenting family traditions, "once in a lifetime" events, and other special moments.

This book is intended to be continually useful over many years. The information contained within will always be of interest to anyone who wishes to use video as a form of personal expression. The concepts, strategies, and techniques should never lose their practicality. We hope that each time you choose to read any section of this book you will come away with new knowledge.

Many of the chapters include worksheets and checklists which are meant to be copied and used each time you go through the necessary steps to plan, organize, and shoot a program. These forms were specially designed to help make the HVP preplanning approach effective for you.

As production specialists, we have developed the HVP approach over the last five years and taught it to hundreds of students in workshops across the country. What makes this plan different from others in this field is that it emphasizes techniques for making complete programs without the need for expensive postproduction editing. In order to produce a complete program with good continuity, preproduction planning is a must. What HVP does for the producer is make it simple to plan, shoot, and view an interesting personal program.

We hope you will enjoy the book, find it a helpful resource, and most of all, "turn on to video" and what it can mean to you as a medium for personal communication.

Pamela Levine, Jeffrey Glasser, Stephen Gach
Authors

TABLE OF CONTENTS

I

ANALYZING THE EVENT

"You need to go and observe a sample
happening, so that you have an idea of
what comprises the event."

CHAPTER 1

ANALYZING THE EVENT

Videotaping--or videographing--requires content planning. Appropriate preplanning insures that you will get what you want, what is important to you. Once an event is under way you have only one chance to record the action. The first six steps (chapters) of this production plan are all focused on preproduction considerations.

One of the first things to do is come to terms with how familiar you are with the event you are covering. Events like birthday parties and weddings usually have a special order and sequence to them. In many cases you need to go and observe a sample happening, so that you have an idea of what comprises the event. In any case, you will go to observe an event with the event analysis sheet that is part of this chapter (see sample, page 9), or you will sit down with this same sheet and write down what the major sequences are, who the major characters of those sequences are, what you feel is important to say about that event, and what interviews you want, so that you can focus on exactly what you would like to capture on tape.

MAJOR SEQUENCES

Carefully observe what is happening. List in chronological order, all the scenes and sequences that occur. Determine the beginning of the event; it may, for example, be sooner than when the guests arrive. Do not be afraid to investigate. It could be something that happens in preparation for the event that actually adds some kind of special understanding to the people, the environment or the event, which should be included.

In order for the program to make sense and to have a focus for the viewers, the tape must have a beginning, middle, and end. This does not mean, of course, that the beginning of the event has to be the start of your tape. You could actually start with the end. If you are videographing a wedding, you could start with the couple dancing or throwing the bouquet, fade down to black, then come up with the bride getting ready for her wedding. But you must know your sequences clearly--what the beginning, middle, and end of the event is--so that you can order your program aesthetically and make a clear statement to the viewer.

If you go to a location to observe an event you are unfamiliar with, you will want to spend your time quietly--removed from the group and observing, not participating. You must be on the outside looking at the event objectively so that you can make choices. Write down everything so that you do not miss any point which at a later date could be important to include in your program. You should listen to people involved in the event. Watch for the kinds of things they find interesting. You can discover these subtleties by being quiet, listening carefully, and observing as much as you can.

An option to going by yourself to observe an event would be to take somebody with you. This could be a person who is going to be a member of your crew, or perhaps a member of your family-- somebody with whom you can discuss the happenings. It can be important to have somebody to "bounce ideas off"--a sounding board. The more input you have, the more complete you can make your approach to presenting the event.

List even what you think is unimportant. You may find that at a later time when you sit down and "brainstorm" (i.e., consider what would make your approach to this event unique to your viewers), you can pull these out as options to pick from.

When you get home, it is time to review the event analysis sheet. Go and sit in a quiet space, and recall the event, adding any additional special emotional times or moments that you feel should be included in the program. For example, these could be reaction shots of family members as the bride and groom kiss at a wedding, or the look on Grandma's face as the child opens up her particular present at a birthday party. These kinds of human insights will give variety and impact to your program. We call these types of visuals "cutaways" or "reaction shots"; they add

4

to the program the special emotions and feelings of people surrounding the event.

If you are doing an event you are very familiar with, and you do not plan to observe it beforehand (i.e., you know exactly what is going to happen), then fill out your event analysis sheet by first thinking about those items that are an integral part of the event. For instance, if you are videographing Thanksgiving dinner, you may want to capture Aunt Jenny in the kitchen with Mom, as she is every year. The kitchen and Aunt Jenny fit so well together that you cannot picture that event without including her in that particular environment. Therefore, it is important to always list the items of a sequence that are predictable and particular to your family, in that way making your program very special, and giving it a point of view.

MAJOR CHARACTERS

Another column on the event analysis sheet is "major characters." This heading refers not only to one star, but perhaps a small number of "mini-stars." These are the people who are important to the event, in addition to the main focus or star of the event. You must weigh carefully who you have designated as the major characters. There should be more than one character who interests you, because at any event there is more than just one person involved. If you were taping a "Sweet Sixteen" with the birthday girl as your star, there would be the mother and father who planned the event, and family members participating in it, whom you would want to include. When taping any event, you should establish as many people there as possible, using cover (wide) shots. You will want that information in years to come, but you will not particularly want to highlight every participant.

As another example, shooting your child's little league team. The major character, of course, would be your child. Other major characters would be the coach (or coaches) and perhaps your immediate family. Then there are the other players on the team. You may just want to introduce them all or have them all wave in a group shot. Or you may want Jimmy's best friend or friends to say why they like being there and what is important to them. What about the parents of all the other kids who are there sitting on the sidelines? Is it important to know why they are there watching their kids? What is it that they like about the game? That would depend on your audience. If you are making the tape for the little league, then you may want to know why the parents came. If you are making the tape for yourself the information is not as important, and you would not consider them major characters requiring an interview.

NEED-TO-KNOW INFORMATION

Another column on the event analysis sheet is headed Need-to-Know information. This consideration is a great help in eliminating the kinds of nice-to-know information which does not provide the strength to move your program forward. Nice-to-know takes up valuable time and can take away from the focus of your program. It is need-to-know that Jimmy the birthday boy and Johnny the best friend have known each other since kindergarten, but only nice-to-know that Johnny arrived with a cast on his foot and how it happened.

You should consider the content and visual focus of every sequence of the event. The focus is determined by the need-to-know information, what it is you want to say about the particular sequence. Let's use the little league game again. Your child is up at bat. What is the content focus? How hard your child is trying? How he is hitting the ball? Do you want a close-up of his face and determination? Is the focus his batting stance and using video to help him improve how he hits? What is the visual focus that supports the content? Do you want to be behind him, catching the whole field, seeing where the ball goes--or do you want to be on the sidelines looking toward him?

In deciding what is the need-to-know information, it is also important to begin thinking of who the different viewing audiences are going to be and what their special interests are. For instance, in taping a little league game, is the tape for your child's benefit, for your own family's enjoyment, or a document for the team. The child will be interested in his every move. You and your family may be interested in your child interacting with the team. But the team will want a visual summary of each major play during the event.

INTERVIEWS

In building family albums, shooting video is not like the old Super 8 days when you pointed the camera at a cover shot of the action and got the person to wave at you. With video, shooting tape is inexpensive; you can actually build in special moments if you take time to analyze what it is you want to say, and where you want to break the action and add depth with interviews. Too many cover shots without in-depth exploration can run on and become very boring.

If you are on vacation videographing your father/husband waterskiing, and it is his favorite sport, you want more than waterskiing, falls, and tricks. You need an interview to record his feelings about skiing, why it is his favorite sport, etc. Interviews give depth and special meaning to sequences and events.

Interviews also personalize the tape, through the emotion shown on faces while people speak and the kinds of words people use to describe their feelings. In home video it is very important to have interviews occur while simple actions are happening. In the case of a birthday party, for instance, when Mother is in the kitchen lighting the candles, be sure to do an interview with her to find out her feelings about the party, the kids, the whole event. It's a simple task that she is doing. Your viewers will be able to "root" very quickly to the visual of the candles being lit, and then focus in on the feelings that she is relating during that interview. This is the type of content planning a good program requires.

There is one sad truth about interviews: if you do not plan for them, once the event is over and everybody disburses you have no opportunity to get those interviews you want. You must plan for interviews or lose them. The best time to get them is between points of action, or during a transition between two sequences. To get that interview you must make arrangements with the interviewee in advance, if possible. You should do some research on the interviews: who should be interviewed in each sequence and what the other members of your family would like to know. There will be other people surrounding you who will give you the information and ideas to ask in the interview. Their input will broaden and add depth to the particular interview, as well as build a variety of questions to ask. Make sure to add this information on your event analysis sheet.

Let's review quickly.

The event analysis sheet must be filled out. Either fill it out after observing an unfamiliar event, or while recalling a familiar one. Put the information in a logical order. The following items should be included while filling out the sheet:

1)   List the major sequences of the event. Organize the sequences to reflect a beginning, middle, and end.

2)   List the major characters of the event. Limit and focus on those characters close to the event and make mini-stars of them.

3)   Designate need-to-know information for each sequence. Do your fact-finding. Ask other members in the family what they would like to include. Think of things that are particular to your family--things that would be important for years to come.

4)   Note the interviews needed.

By filling out the event analysis sheet and giving it careful consideration, you will be able to see where you can aesthetically add information and visuals to make your story more interesting. The worksheet makes organizing your program simple. It takes all the guesswork out of "where do I begin?" and "how should I state my message?" It gives you a foundation for building your tape.

SAMPLE

EVENT ANALYSIS SHEET

EVENT _____ Child's Birthday Party _____ DATE _____ 1-31-83 _____

MAJOR SEQUENCES	MAJOR CHARACTERS	NEED-TO-KNOW INFORMATION	INTERVIEWS NEEDED
Decorate room	Mom and younger sister	1. Age of child 2. Plan for party 3. Significance of decorations	Mom sister
Guests arrive	Grandparents Aunt & Uncle Special friends	1. All the guests arriving	Grandparents Aunt Tilly
Children playing	Birthday child	1. Games 2. Talking together	
Mom lighting candles	Mom	1. Feelings about children and party	Mom
Cake arrives/	Mom and Birthday child	1. Birthday song & children singing 2. Birthday child's face blowing out candles 3. Other children	
Open presents	Birthday child	1. Child opening presents 2. Child's excitement	Birthday child
Guests leaving	The guests as a group	1. What they enjoyed about the party	Child's favorite friends

EVENT ANALYSIS SHEET

EVENT_____   DATE_____

MAJOR SEQUENCES	MAJOR CHARACTERS	NEED-TO-KNOW INFORMATION	INTERVIEWS NEEDED

II

PLANNING THE PRODUCTION

"Brainstorming is both creative and fun,
but it must be properly organized."

CHAPTER 2

PLANNING THE PRODUCTION

The second step of HVP is to plan your production and generate a program outline. There are four subjects we will discuss in coming up with your program plan:

1)   Knowing your audience
2)   Audio
3)   Lighting
4)   Brainstorming

It is necessary to consider the first three in order to effectively organize the program plan which happens during (4) brainstorming.

KNOW YOUR AUDIENCE

Having completed analyzing the event, you should now think in terms of the audience and the length of your tape. What is it you want to accomplish with the audience who is going to be viewing your tape? If they are immediate family members they will have a greater motivation level and attention span than if they are friends. Family members will overlook problems with your production techniques (shaky camerawork or loss-of-focus) and still enjoy the program. They will want to see every bit of a scene you have, all the details and more. On the other hand, friends will want to be entertained in a different fashion. They expect what they see on their TV. They are impatient with bad technique and drawn out action. They want the program to get to the point.

While there is a certain amount of organization for the two different audiences that can be done in setting up different viewing scripts, still you must decide who the program is basically for--yourself and immediate family, or other people. This choice will determine how you plan the sequences and shoot the production.

For an immediate family audience, sequences should be designed in more detail and more time should be spent at a given location and with each subject. Interviews can have more depth and action can be revealed more slowly. For audience other than your "video family," no program should be longer than 15 minutes. People are used to broadcast programming with commercial breaks every 10 minutes and will become restless if the program lingers too long.

Now, before you can brainstorm, there are two areas that you should understand better. These are essential to good programming, but are rarely discussed in home video equipment manuals: audio and lighting.

AUDIO

As television producers, we believe that good audio can save bad video; but good video cannot save bad audio. You can have the most terrific video in the world, but if the audio is indistinguishable, or has a bad buzz in it, no one will pay attention to the program. However, if you have good, "hot" audio, and the video is questionable (e.g., a shake in it, loss of picture, glare, or the picture is a bit washed-out), the audio can hold the program together. Good sound reinforces the reality of the video portion of your program and often saves questionable video. Poor quality audio distracts the viewer.

By understanding the pickup pattern and features of each microphone relative to the placement requirement of the recording situation, it will be easy to choose the appropriate mike and accessories you need for each family event.

With video, use only low impedance mikes. Low impedance mikes offer better reception and higher quality sound than high impedance mikes. These mikes can be used with long extension cables without producing a buzz or picking up radio signals. They are designed to be used with video equipment.

Types of Mikes

The two basic mikes used with HVP are condenser mikes and dynamics. The condenser microphone requires batteries. It is known for its crisp, clean sound over a wide frequency range and reproduces the human voice exceptionally well. The best type of condenser mike to use is called a "back electret" condenser mike. Remember, with battery operated microphones you cannot leave a battery stored inside the microphone. This will drain the battery and give weak audio recording. Every time you use that mike, remove the battery when you are finished. In addition, if you leave the battery inside the microphone and if exposed to extreme temperature, the battery is going to leak, damaging the mike. If you are going on location with battery operated mikes, be sure to take backup batteries. They are inexpensive and can be changed on a regular basis. Most mike batteries offer 100 hours of running time. When a battery starts to lose power, you still will hear sound through an earphone, but unless you have a mixer to give a meter reading, it is difficult to tell if you are losing sound quality. It follows that you might tape a very important event and not have enough volume in your sound when playing back the tape. We always use a fresh battery for each new shoot.

Dynamic is the other microphone type, and the most exciting in terms of current innovation, approaching audio reproduction levels of condenser formats. The dynamic does not require battery operation. It plugs directly into your system. It is a very durable and rugged mike. We have seen dynamic mikes still working that have teeth marks in them from use with young children. We recommend using dynamic mikes whenever possible.

Microphone Pickup Patterns

There are essentially two microphone pickup patterns you have to be concerned with. One is called the unidirectional pattern, and the other, the omnidirectional pattern. Unidirectional means one direction, with sound picked up primarily from the front (aimed directly at the sound source) with minimum pickup from the sides. There are some basic unidirectional mikes you should own. The most unidirectional mike available is a shotgun. It will give you good directional pickup at a range of 10 to 15 feet. If you were videographing a group with interaction and response, traditionally there would be multiple mikes--one mike for every three people--with cable running into several audio mixers (see audio accessories page 35--"Mixers"). You would work very hard trying to get the right mike turned on and up at the right time, while taking down the others to eliminate sneezes and coughs. The shotgun microphone, on the other hand, can be mounted on your camera (many cameras today come with one already attached), and as quick as you can videograph the person responding, the directional signal from the mike homes in and picks up the right person without extraneous sounds on either side. A shotgun mike is usually held slightly above the subject pointing downward, because the audio comes up.

A situation may arise, however, where a shotgun mike cannot move fast enough to cover the action and several mikes are needed (e.g., a group interacting at a large table). Since your tape deck has only one audio input, an audio mixer is necessary (see page 35--"Mixers"). An inexpensive audio mixer has input for up to four mikes with an output cable for plugging into your VCR.

Another type of unidirectional mike is a cardioid. This is the most ideal type of microphone used for interviews where two or more people are talking back and forth. It has a heartshape pickup pattern (see page 21) canceling most extraneous noise and is very sensitive to the speakers within its range. Working distance is most effective at 1 to 2 feet from the sound source. Cardioid mikes are the workhorse of the interview situation. They are usually hand-held, but sometimes used on a desk or stand. On location, they cancel out enough frontal noise so you can hear the interview and still get a background sense of presence of the environment.

One other mike you might want to consider in the unidirectional area is a parabolic microphone. It is commonly used at large sporting events such as football games. It uses a plastic parabolic dish with an inverted directional mike and will pick up sound from about 125 feet. The parabolic is a very directional mike designed for long distance, and is ideal for sporting events such as little league, where you wish to pick up sound on the playing field.

The second basic pickup pattern for microphones is omni-directional. It has a pickup pattern of a sphere--360°--which means it picks up from all directions simultaneously, with a slight preference for the direction in which the mike is pointed. If used improperly, it can be dangerous to your audio quality. For example, many built-in camera mikes are omnidirectional. With these mikes, it is common to pick up the breathing of the cameraperson, a plane overhead, cars passing by, and other unwanted sound with a low tinny quality. Plugging in an external mike to the mike-in jack on the VCR will automatically defeat the camera mike. If you have an absence of ambient sound, then an omnidirectional mike will work. It has a pickup range of about 8 feet. Basically, the only omnidirectional microphone that we would recommend is a lavalier microphone, often called a lapel mike because it attaches to your clothing. The lavalier is useful in isolating a singular source, and allowing for considerable soft physical movement (i.e., walking around, not jumping or exercise) while still picking up sound. With this omnidirectional lavalier you have 360° pickup. When fixed to the chest, half the pickup pattern is blocked, but still allows for 180° pickup. Talent (subject) can walk around, have his hands free, move his head and still get good sound pickup with extraneous noise behind blocked by the body. It can also be helpful in covering several voices where there is little extraneous sound if hung overhead and just out of camera sight (within 5 feet of talent). The 360° pickup pattern can cover a very useful area.

Selection and Placement

It is important you choose the right type of mike with the correct pickup pattern for a particular situation. If you are doing interviews in a quiet environment, a dynamic or condenser mike with an omnidirectional mike is going to work. But if you are shooting in areas with a lot of ambient noise, such as outside near traffic or in a cafeteria, you are going to need a unidirectional microphone to achieve quality sound.

If the room has a smooth ceiling, polished floor, and paneled walls, sound will bounce extensively. This means you should choose unidirectional microphones and place them close to the sound source. If mike visibility is not desired, and considerable ambient sound and bounce is present, then use a shotgun mike. For panel discussion with three or more people seated in a semicircle where mike visibility is allowable, ambient noise is at a minimum, and some sound absorption material exists in the environment (i.e., drapes, carpet, acoustical ceiling), an omnidirectional mike on a stand equidistant from the subjects or hung from the ceiling may be used. If, however, sound bounce and ambient noise do exist, then several cardioid mikes on stands or lavaliers tied to a mixer would be advisable.

For field interviews with two or more people in an environment with considerable ambient noise and bounce, use a hand-held dynamic mike with a cardioid pickup pattern, to minimize extraneous sound. Remember dynamic mikes do not require batteries, are the most rugged type, and have less handling noise than condenser mikes.

Most portable video cassette recorders (VCRs) are equipped with Automatic Gain Control (AGC), which is designed to automatically equalize and maintain various sound levels being recorded. Some of the newer VCRs also have adjustable volume controls to ride audio manually. In the absence of a strong incoming audio signal (e.g., a very long pause), the AGC can cause the VCR to amplify unwanted background sound. AGC is not discriminating and too often picks up only the loudest noises. If possible on your VCR use the manual audio position and defeat AGC where audio levels change significantly throughout the sequence.

In summary, to determine which microphone you need for your taping in relation to pickup pattern and placement, always analyze:

  * Number of people to be covered
  * Amount and direction of subject movement
  * Microphone visibility
  * Acoustical conditions
  * Ambient noise factors

MICROPHONE PICKUP PATTERNS

Unidirectional
(cardioid)

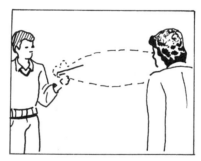

Unidirectional
(shotgun)

Omnidirectional
(lavalier)

LIGHTING

Lighting is one of the most important areas in home video production. First, you should not become intimidated by the subject. If you relax and have fun with it, lighting is both simple and logical. There are two basic principles. The first basic principle of lighting is to get enough light for the camera to reproduce the image effectively. The second principle is using lights to express a feeling, mood, aesthetic; adding depth and dimension to the program. We will first review the basic lighting techniques necessary for good recording of most home video programs. This will include the use of "back" light and "fill" light. Second, we will expand the basic use of these lights to achieve aesthetics of lighting. This will include the use of 3-point lighting and more detailed lighting setup. Due to time, budget and crew limitations, and spontaneity of the event, you will not always be able to apply all these rules of aesthetic lighting. Keep in mind, however, the following techniques are important to understand and grow into as you develop your HVP skills.

First, as a home video producer you should focus on getting enough light so the camera can adequately see the picture. Outdoors there is almost always enough light to satisfy the camera. Indoors this light is called base light. In most cases, it means using portable floods (also called "fills" or "soft lights") to bring up the general lighting of an indoor location to a level suitable to shoot and get good picture resolution. These could be quartz lights or clamp-on floods (the hardware store variety). Sometimes raising the wattage of table, floor, and ceiling lamps in the room will also provide a better base light situation.

There are two rules we suggest you always use to determine light quality:

1)   Look at the subject(s) and area in question, either on the viewfinder of the camera or preferably on the TV set. The TV should be properly set for brightness, contrast, color and hue by tuning in a good broadcast program and manually adjusting the knobs. Set "hue" to achieve good flesh tones. Professionals use a color bar tape playing back onto the TV. A color bar tape

can be purchased from a production house or video dealer. In preparing a taping session, set your controls once. Using your TV as a reference while you shoot, you will be able to see if areas are too dark and losing detail or too bright and washing out.

2) Invest in an inexpensive light meter that reads footcandles (standard measurement of light intensity) and use it to measure the overall room light against the suggested amount of light needed for a good picture on your camera (usually stated in footcandles on the camera specification sheet). The light meter and the TV monitor will tell you if you need to add base light to a scene.

Before we continue talking about base light, there is an important concept we should review. The television camera takes the best pictures when it is focusing on scenes with moderate contrast and with simple texture. In television production, there is a very important moderate contrast rule that you should consider. For good camera pictures, you should always try to achieve a moderate contrast relationship between four elements: skin tone of major talent, clothing, backgrounds, and graphic material. Thus, when choosing a scene as background for your talent try to avoid:

* bright, distracting backgrounds
* heavy, unwanted shadows
* chrome, shiny metals, darkwood furniture or paneling
* loud, bold patterns on walls, drapery, furniture (herringbones, bold plaids)
* extreme colors (e.g., bright reds, yellow)
* white to black contrasts

All of these items must be taken into consideration in dealing with the environment and learning how to use light. Extreme contrast relationships cause the camera to resolve a picture that is washed-out in some areas, dark in others. Detail is lost. The picture may also be muddy or noisy (snowy). Too much bright red or yellow or white can cause skin tone to go yellow. Too much bold pattern or detail can cause vibration (moire, patternshake) in the picture. (A good example is when Johnny Carson wears a bold plaid suit on TV. Not too much problem on the

23

cover shot of him. But when the camera zooms in tight on him
you can see a vibration coming off of his lapel or elbow.)

Therefore, before you decide on base light, you must first
understand the contrast relationship of the elements in the
environment you want to light.

When you add base light, remember that dark colors absorb more
light, while light colors reflect more. For example, when lighting
a living room with dark furniture and white walls and ceiling,
more light (flood, soft, fill) should be concentrated on the
furniture area and less on the walls and ceiling. In the case of
low white ceilings, however, you could bounce fill light off the
ceiling, which would brighten the room areas to which the bounce
light is directed. Try to keep windows behind the camera and
out of the camera's composition. They are so bright your
subject(s) will become a silhouette. Normally three floods (each
500-750 watts) or one to two soft fills (each 500-1000 watts) may
be used to bring up the base level in a dark, indoor location.
Remember, you can use 150-300 watt bulbs in your room lamps to
up the base light as well.

Once the adequate base light level for camera needs is established
(remember light meter and TV monitor), aesthetics are the next
priority. Indoor aesthetics usually apply some application of the
standard lighting formula called 3-point lighting. Outdoors,
reflectors may be used. Aesthetic lighting techniques are
designed for more sophisticated shoots and require more control
over the environment than the average home event allows. The
rules are important for you to understand, however, for
expanding your knowledge level of general lighting approaches.

There are two basic types of lighting fixtures used in television.
One is the flood (fill, soft) which is also used in base lighting.
These lights offer soft, low contrast illumination. They minimize
shadow, and allow for good subject movement. They have a wide
beam. The second light is a spot. It offers high intensity
output with relatively small size. The light is hard, directive,
dramatic, and produces contrast similar to the sun. The spot
highlights detail and produces hard shadows.

The 3-point lighting system consists of a key (spot) light, a fill light, and a back (spot) light: a combination of the basic fixtures. The key light is the strongest light. It creates a harsh, directional light on one side of the subject. It is often called the modeling or primary light source. It is very concentrated and gives the illusion of dimension. It is usually hung or placed on a light stand in a position 45° up and over from the subject to the left or right side of the camera. The second light is the fill. Its purpose is to soften the effect of the key light by filling in the shadows, which gives a certain softness and rounding out to the subject. Often, on location with many subjects and movement, the only extra lighting will be fill. The fill is a soft diffused light which minimizes shadow. It is usually hung or placed on a light stand in a position 30° up and 45° over from the subject on the opposite side of the camera from the key lights. The last light in 3-point lighting is the back light which separates the subject(s) from the background. It is usually a hard (spot) light similar to the key, and hung above and behind the subject. (For a better understanding of the relationship and placement of fixtures in 3-point lighting see the following diagrams.)

3-POINT LIGHTING

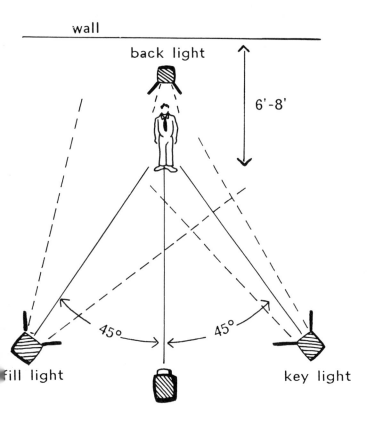

wall

back light

6'-8'

45°   45°

fill light   key light

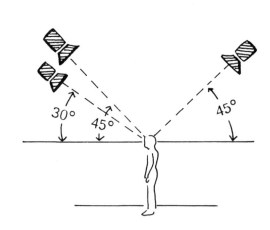

30°   45°   45°

3-POINT LIGHTING APPROACH

Type of Light (Quartz)	Function	Effect	Intensity	Placement
KEY	Hard primary light	Simulates sun	Use lamps of 500-1000W	45° above & to one side of subject
	Concentrated spot	Models subjects	Strongest light	Dead center to soften heavy features
		Creates hard shadows	Determines intensity of other lights	Lower for deep-set eyes or problem skin
		Dramatic		
BACK	Hard primary light	Separates subject from background	500W-1000W same as KEY or up to 1½ more intensity than KEY	45° above subject
	Concentrated spot	Adds dimension & depth		Directly opposite to camera or diagonal to KEY or FILL
		Rims hair, shoulders of people		
FILL	Secondary light	Softens, reduces hard KEY shadows	500-1000W ½ less intensity of KEY	45° to opposite side of subject from KEY
	Diffused			30° above subject
	Broad-beam	Adds depth, form to face		
	Flood			

To avoid harsh shadows on walls (particularly in a small room), use soft fill light and bring your subject(s) as far away from the wall as possible toward the center of the room. Remember the viewer's eyes will always be directed to the brightest element on the screen. Keep the most important elements in your sequence the brightest.

Lights require substantial electrical power. During location checkouts, pay particular attention to power sources at each location. AC outlets have definite power limitations. A single circuit supplies about 1500 watts (15 amps). Do not overload one circuit. Remember your VCR and cameras pull power, too. Generally it is best to divide the lights between two or three lines if they are available. Have adequate AC extension cord in case that extra circuit is in another room. Tape the cord to carpet so no one trips.

After your lights are set use your TV to check all areas appearing on camera. Have someone walk through those areas and watch the TV. Readjust your lights if necessary. Tape the effect of different lighting arrangements and compare them on playback. This is how you will learn to light.

If you are outdoors, you can still utilize aesthetic lighting. Buy several large pieces of cardboard. Tack crumpled tin foil on to the cardboard and use it as a reflector (a white or silver card can also serve). If sunlight is coming in behind the subject, for example, it would serve as a back light. With the use of a reflector in front of the subject, the sun could also be used as a key light. The reflector can bounce the sunlight back onto the face of a subject, providing good illumination. Reflector boards can also be used to eliminate harsh background shadows by bouncing light into areas behind the subjects. Sunlight produces great color quality. Cameras love it! Sharp, vivid detail is possible without the use of artificial lights.

Common problems to look out for are overly bright backgrounds and bright blue skies. Under such conditions, the "auto-iris" in your camera can overcompensate for the high contrast by darkening the video picture (remember the moderate contrast rule). When you see the camera picture darken rapidly (in your viewfinder or TV), zoom in and tighten your shot on the outdoor subject to lose the bright contrast background of the picture. Or, turn your camera and subject around so that the overly bright sky, for instance, is behind the camera.

We recommend that every home video producer invest in a simple lighting kit and accessories (see page 37) that are portable and rugged. This should include approximately four to six light fixtures between base and 3-point considerations. Please keep in mind, however, that we are giving you techniques to grow into-- if you have the time, interest, budget, and crew. There are plenty of home producers who work solely with one or two floods, quartz or incandescent (some even use a sun gun attached to their camera), and are satisfied with their results. Limiting yourself to one or two lights makes for harsher video. It is important to know your options and how to improve the picture if you desire. The use of base and 3-point lighting together opens up those options to you. Certainly if lighting fixtures present a problem to you, another option is to shoot outdoors where fixtures are generally not required.

LIGHTING HOME INTERVIEWS INEXPENSIVELY

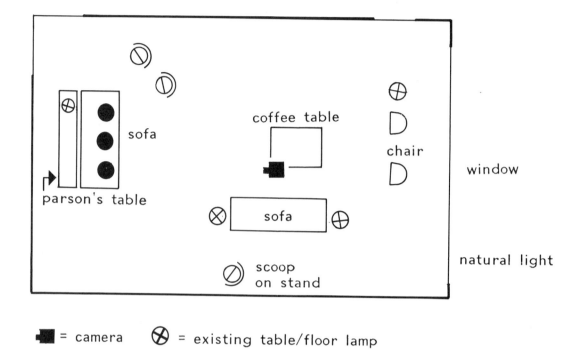

= camera   ⊗ = existing table/floor lamp

● = talent   ◌ = inexpensive metal scoop light
                      bought at photo/hardware store

Lots of things can be done to increase the existing base light of a room conveniently and inexpensively. Replace existing 25- to 60-watt bulbs in the table lamps with 300-watt photo flood bulbs to more than triple the amount of light. Then add several inexpensive metal "scoops" that use 300- to 600-watt photo flood lights. These scoops can sit on inexpensive stands or can be held by clamps to existing shelves or cabinet doors.

The "scoops" and photo flood bulbs can be bought at any hardware or photo supply store.

This light should easily coexist with any other artificial light you might introduce.

BRAINSTORMING

In designing your program plan you are now ready to consider brainstorming. Brainstorming is both creative and fun, but it must be properly organized. The primary steps of the brainstorming session are: idea generation, idea evaluation, idea commitment, and preparation of the program outline.

The first step of brainstorming is the idea-generation session. What you are trying to accomplish is to encourage those people involved in the home video shoot to think of ways to visualize the items on the event analysis sheet. The session is usually held with your crew and all participate equally. The producer should lead the group through idea generation and not pass judgment on the participants' ideas. It usually takes about 30 minutes or so, depending on the length of your event analysis sheet. The ideas should be listed on a blackboard or large piece of paper, so everybody can see.

Use the event analysis sheet from Chapter 1, which outlines the sequences of the event, the major characters, the need-to-know information and interviews.

During idea generation it usually takes 10 minutes to get people past traditional roles. So, if you are the "head of household" of the family, and you are working with your kids, it is going to take you 10 minutes of encouraging them to throw in ideas, to participate. It is the kind of beginning where you are saying to them, "How would you treat that sequence?" "Come on, let's hear what you have to say about that interview!" "Gee, that's a great idea! Let's write that down!" Everything gets written down during idea generation. Nothing gets judged.

Usually the second 10 minutes of the idea generation session is very exciting. If you've done a good warm-up, people are "into it." You are pulling ideas out of them. Everything's getting written down. The last 10 minutes is a windup. You are encouraging them to come up with that last idea or treatment. Even the most bizarre idea should be written down. In this first step of brainstorming, the more creative the minds you have participating, the more different the points of view you will hear. The greater the variety of input to the brainstorming session, the more possible approaches and options you will have in the second step, idea evaluation.

The second step of brainstorming is to evaluate those ideas realistically against what you are capable of doing, what your budget will allow, and what your equipment can perform (including audio and lights). You are also considering the program length and the major target audience. In this step you are eliminating those ideas that do not fit within your capabilities. Use the brainstorm consideration sheet (on page 33) to perform idea evaluation. If you have a negative response, the idea will not fit within your capabilities. If the event is one where participants have a vested interest (family, friends, etc.), then as the producer you may want to involve everyone in this second step of idea evaluation. If not, thank them for their input and do the evaluation yourself.

The third step of brainstorming is to look at the ideas that have been left after the first elimination, reconsider them, choose carefully, and commit yourself to a program outline. A program outline is a treatment of how your video piece is going to look and sound. During this third step of final commitment you prepare the program outline by listing in order on paper the basic information, location, visual and audio treatment.

Now that you have an idea of your program outline, you should begin to rethink the people-power necessary to produce the program. Some events you wish to cover will be quite involved, with perhaps many sequences and locations, and a lot of people in attendance. For large events such as a wedding or baseball game, you should think of using a crew of about three to four family members or friends to help you move quickly and without too much time lost from location to location to shoot the action. In other cases some events will be simpler with fixed locations and fewer participants--perhaps a more quiet, intimate happening such as a family dinner. In such a situation it's probably wiser to use a small crew (one or two) to help you, making sure to move quietly and not become a distraction to the event.

BRAINSTORM CONSIDERATIONS

1. Can this sequence be shot within our time limits?

2. Do we have time to do proper preproduction planning?

3. Does the sequence present difficult lighting, audio, or staging problems?

4. Do we have the proper equipment?
   * Camera/VCR
   * Sound equipment
   * AC/DC outlets/batteries
   * Lights
   * Graphics

5. Can we get permission to use the proposed locations?

6. Can we get the necessary talent and crew?

7. Can this sequence be made within our budget?

8. Will this treatment appeal to our target audience?

9. Is it the proper length to maintain viewer attention/interest?

10. Fill in your own:

AUDIO ACCESSORIES

* <u>Mixers</u>--used for combining two or more sound sources. After selecting and blending various sounds, the mixer supplies a composite output to the VCR. Buy portable mixers that have AC capability for postproduction use. Good mixers have VU meters for monitoring the volume level of the mixed sound; they allow impedance selection, and they allow various other sources to be connected (e.g., mikes, tape decks, stereo amplifiers, etc.). Each input should have its own volume control (pot) as well as the master volume control.

* <u>Microphones</u>--extra mikes are not accessories. Think of them as necessities. Lavalier, hand-held, and shotgun mikes are important if you shoot "documentary" style or conduct many interviews.

* <u>Extra cables for mikes</u>--long lengths of cable allow more freedom in positioning the interviewer (or other talent) away from the VCR.

* <u>Adaptor connectors</u>--make it possible for your mikes to plug into virtually any system's audio inputs and allow you additional flexibility in your use of auxiliary audio systems (e.g., stereo amps, tape decks, mixers).

* <u>Wind filters</u>--usually a foam cover that fits over the top of the mike to reduce unwanted noise.

* <u>Headset/earphone</u>--invaluable in determining volume and quality of an incoming sound source. It also alerts the VCR operator to the absence of audio.

* <u>Boom/fish pole</u>--a telescoping pole used for nonvisible overhead placement of mike to talent when close distancing is required.

* <u>Audio tape recorder</u>--used to record ambient noise at locations, interviews to be used as a narration track, and music.

LIGHTING ACCESSORIES

BUY PORTABLE QUARTZ LIGHTS (packaged in a kit of three or four); SUPPLEMENT WITH THE FOLLOWING ACCESSORIES:

* Barn doors--hinged metal flaps on fixture that direct the spread of illumination and control beam direction. Moving barn doors can eliminate unwanted shadows.

* Scrims--a screen, metal or spun-glass, placed in front of lamp to soften and reduce brightness. Several scrims can be used at once. Spun-glass can be cut to size to cover only a portion of a fixture to soften a bright portion of the scene when extreme contrast exists.

* Light stands--buy lightweight metal stands, with a strong base and sturdy legs. C-clamps and Gaffer Grips are helpful to position small portable lighting fixtures in hard-to-reach areas. They fasten the fixtures to any sturdy object or surface.

* Reflector boards--inexpensive, yet ideal for soft fill light (especially on the face) when shooting outdoors on a bright day. Diffuse and balance sunlight, fill in shadows. Use cardboard--white, silver, or covered with crumpled aluminum foil.

* Softlights--special portable fixtures; 1500W collapsible units used in raising the general illumination of a scene. Virtually shadowless.

* Sun gun--battery-powered light source with rapid charge, designed to be hand-held or attached to the camera. Acts as major source of subject illumination. Provides 25 to 60 minutes of light depending on lamp wattage. If possible, general illumination should be no less than half-intensity of sun gun to avoid harsh, contrasty look of subject. This type of lighting gives a hard, contrasty light.

* <u>Extra lamps</u>--different wattage for fixtures.

* <u>Basic floods</u>--buy at hardware store with 150-300 watt bulbs.

* <u>Neutral density filter</u>--useful outside in bright sunlight. It reduces scene brightness. Can buy at photo store.

III

CHECKING THE LOCATION

"An instant camera will help you recall
vital information once you leave the
scene."

CHAPTER 3

CHECKING THE LOCATION

As a home video producer, you will find there are going to be times in your family's video experience when you have special events to cover, such as a wedding or a very important party, or perhaps a very special interview with a member of your family. It is necessary for covering these special events well that you expand your preplanning. We have made a point throughout the book that the more you can plan as you lead up to the shoot, the better you are going to be in terms of capturing the information you want, and the more enjoyable it will be. You should know as much as possible about the location for your shoot. Checking the location has always been a very important consideration for commercial producers. It is the same for home producers. In order to check the location, there are a variety of concepts you should first understand. These concepts focus on how the eye and the TV camera see things differently. They cover the subjects of field of view, aspect ratio, simulation, spatial relationships, and contrast ratio.

FIELD OF VIEW

See the image as it appears on the television screen. When you look at an environment with your eye and then take a picture with your camera, it is going to look quite different on the screen than you thought. What was a wide expanse to your eye will have the peripheral areas cropped when it appears on the television screen, as seen by your camera lens.

One of the keys to visualizing a sequence is being able to make the transition from what you see with your eye to the way the image appears on the television screen.

The field of view of the eye is about 180°. The field of view of the normal television lens is about 45°.

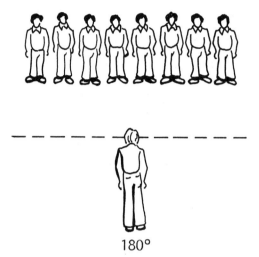

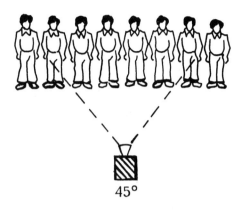

The eye roots to the horizon, seeing a broad peripheral span with a limited vertical field of view. The TV camera and screen images everything in a 3x4 aspect ratio.

ASPECT RATIO

Aspect ratio is a height and width measurement of an object or visual space. In television, the aspect ratio is almost a cube, three units high by four units across. The aspect ratio of what the eye sees is more of a long rectangle, one unit high by four units across. The human eye views most objects in relation to a horizontal plane. The following drawings illustrate the same image as seen by the eye and the TV screen.

"eye"   "TV screen"

Compose all video pictures in the 3x4 aspect ratio of the TV screen.

SIMULATION

The camera tends to generalize detail. Fine detail taken for granted by the eye tends to lose definition on the screen and appears cluttered. If you try to deal with a large or wide amount of detailed information, by the time it reaches the television screen not only is the picture going to be cut off on the sides, but the visuals will seem quite complex. The viewer in turn will have difficulty in focusing on what is important. To avoid this complexity it is necessary to simulate a given scene rather than try to duplicate all that we see with our eyes. This is accomplished by choosing the major elements of the environment and including only them in the picture. For example, in a living room, if you attempted to show in a cover shot all of the chairs, couches, tables, lamps, pictures, knickknacks, and details of the furnishings of that room, they would not be resolved well by the television camera. However, the side of a couch, the edge of a coffee table, and perhaps the edge of a picture on the wall behind the couch would be enough to simulate that room.

You need to think also about how living spaces are arranged. If you think about the way people sit in a room with each other, you realize how people tend to space things on a horizontal level, in keeping with that 1x4 aspect ratio the eye sees. To simulate a normal environment for television it then becomes necessary to move furniture around in a given location to achieve more of the 3x4 proportion for the camera to see. It may even be necessary to physically remove items from a scene, if the picture seems too cluttered in the viewfinder or on the television screen.

Sometimes you are shooting on location and are suddenly in the midst of a cluttered background or environment and unable to physically remove items from the scene. At that moment, it is through choice of camera angle and the size of the shot that you must simplify the picture for the viewer. For example, using a zoomed-in camera shot, a close-up lens, or a long distance between the camera and the subject will all cause a complex background to go out of focus and be less prominent.

Television is a people medium requiring a minimum of background, or environmental materials. You use just a few objects to give an impression of the scene, rather than all of the real life objects, which would be distracting to the viewer. Television is a close-up medium. It gives the illusion of intimacy. The viewer looks at the screen, sees a family member or friend being interviewed, and experiences direct communication with that individual on a very personal level. Home video then can become even more of an intimate medium than commercial TV. You can enhance this ability by the types of shots, interviews, and scenes you choose to handle in your video programs. Keep in mind that wide shots or pans on a wide-angle shot are used to establish the viewer, rather than to show fine detail. A wide shot of a living room or of a scene in a meadow will simply set up the viewer for what is to follow in the next close-up or introspective scene.

SPATIAL RELATIONSHIPS

You create the illusion of depth by putting objects in the foreground and background of the shooting environment. As we consider the aspect ratio of a 3x4 TV picture with limited horizontal field of view and detail, we must also consider the spatial relationship of the subject and objects that the camera sees in a chosen composition. Television is a flat medium. The illusion of depth must be created. If you have a person in an interview situation, you could, for instance, in arranging the scene do something as simple as putting a plant or a small table in front, a person in the middle, and a picture in the back.

Many times the placement of a few simple items in the scene, enables you to create a sense of depth for the viewer. If we go back to our living room example, where we are moving furniture around to create a 3x4 proportion and also removing items from the scene to eliminate clutter, then we should also be aware of creating a sense of depth by the placement of the furniture, people, and accessories in that same environment. This feeling of depth may be present to the eye, but lacking when the image appears on the 2-dimensional screen, especially if the room was initially set up on the horizon--as most spaces are for the eye's natural aspect ratio.

Often, as mentioned in simulation, there is not the opportunity to move furniture around to create the illusion of depth. You must quickly size up the space and choose which position and angle you should take with the camera to best enable you to obtain an illusion of depth and avoid a horizontal composition. Just telling your talent, "could you please move over there," allows you to change your camera angle and achieve the appropriate composition and aspect ratio for the television screen.

Another consideration is the space limitations between objects and people. When a camera videographs a scene, because of the narrow field of view of television, the space between objects and people becomes greatly exaggerated on the screen. If you go back into the living room and look at the arrangement of furniture, you will notice a lot of empty space there. This is fine for daily living and the way the human eye sees things. If you were taping an interview, however, things would appear much further apart on the screen. It would be necessary to close up the empty space to fit into the limited horizontal range of the TV camera. This could be accomplished by moving furniture and people closer together.

When you move people too close together, however, in order to fill up empty spaces, this can create another problem involving social distancing. People get very uncomfortable when they are too close to each other. Their "social space" is violated. Therefore, you must place furniture and/or people with safety distance in mind. What television producers do to fit people into the 3x4 aspect ratio of the TV screen is to make use of angles and depth. This blocking achieves good "tight" composition for the camera and still maintains adequate safety distances between subjects. The choice is to position subjects on either side of an inverted "V" or "L" shape (most TV talk shows use this method). Then shoot the subjects from an angle either left or right of center. The angular placement of talent and camera allows for enough space between talent so they still can feel far enough apart and not threatened. When viewed on a TV screen, it appears that the subjects are at a normal distance from each other.

When you become more familiar in dealing with angles and space, blocking out scenes on location will become second nature. You will just naturally block the position of your camera and the angle of its relationship to the subject, without having to stop the scene and disturb its spontaneity.

CONTRAST RATIO

Another area you must consider in the environment is the contrast relationship or contrast ratio of the elements present. Remember, in Chapter 2, we talked about the moderate contrast rule. The same rule applies when checking the location. To review, there are four elements that should be considered in trying to achieve a moderate contrast relationship so that the camera reproduces good color pictures. They are skin tone of major talent, clothing, backgrounds, and graphic materials.

For example, the television camera may see a very bright or "hot" element in the picture, such as a white shirt (or if indoors, an uncovered window), and as the camera adjusts electronically to deal with this intensity the contrast ratio of all the other elements in the picture becomes extreme. The lights remain light, but the darks become darker. Detail is lost in the darker parts of the picture and is washed-out or bleeds into the lighter parts, especially skin tones. If you want everything on the television screen to be seen by the viewer, then you must keep a moderate contrast ratio. The brightest area should be no more than four or five times brighter than the darkest area (use a light meter to measure). If you keep that kind of contrast ratio when you begin to shoot or when you add light to a scene, you will be in good shape.

If you choose environmental situations where your brightest area is thirty to forty times brighter than your darkest area, such as a person indoors standing in front of a doorway open to the outside, then the result will be a silhouette in front of a washed-out background. Therefore, if one of your sequences involves shooting guests arriving at a daytime party, passing from outdoors to indoors, the contrast ratio must be applied. An approach would be to be outside with your camera, videographing the host/hostess greeting the people outside on the walkway as they arrive. When you are outside greeting the subjects, there is an equal amount of light in the background and on the subject, all generated from the same outside source, the sun. The contrast ratio is minimized. Another alternative is to stand under open shade, which eliminates harsh shadows.

In another example, a very dark-skinned person placed in front of a light wall would be a problem for the camera to render appropriately. The light background would tend to cause the camera to adjust electronically to the light tones, thus darkening all of the features on the dark-skinned person. Instead, a moderate contrast background such as a medium blue background or perhaps a brick wall should be chosen to complement the skin tone of that dark person. By the same token, a very fair-skinned person placed in front of a dark wall would also be problematic.

If you are on location spontaneously shooting a subject and find your background to be in extreme contrast, there are two solutions. One, change the size of your shot. You can choose to move in closer on the subject and eliminate the high contrast background. This will, in turn, bring up the features of the

47

subject you are videographing. Two, change the angle of your shot. By moving your camera to one side or the other of your subject (at least 45°) you may be able to shift the background to one of a moderate contrast relationship with your subject.

Another important element in talking about contrast ratio is clothing. As mentioned earlier, a dark-skinned person in a white T-shirt would present a problem. Again, facial detail would be lost. The option would be to move in and lose as much of the clothing as possible, or suggest he/she change to a moderate contrast piece of clothing in relationship to the skin tone. It is not unusual to ask the people with whom you are going to be shooting video to come dressed in a particular type of clothing. For instance, red does not show up well on a home video camera. Generally whites and blacks are avoided as well. Herringbones, large plaids, houndstooth make the picture on the screen vibrate. In addition, bold stripes and patterns can cause picture smear. All should be avoided if possible.

The best colors to deal with in television for clothing, backgrounds, and graphic materials are shades of blue, green, brown, mauve, mustard, gold, khaki, rose, and rust. The cameras can deal somewhat with jewelry, props, and signage (street signs, billboards, and other such graphic symbols) providing they are not too shiny or reflective. Notice in your camera viewfinder when you are shooting, if there are any "hot" spots or reflective spots that are smearing in the picture.

It is important to emphasize that, while you cannot always control the situation, these points of information should act as signals to you. Your options are to try to physically remove the item from the scene, lose it by zooming in, or change your angle so that it is no longer reflective or visible.

The following chart should be a good review of how the eye and TV camera see things differently.

COMPARISON OF EYE AND TV CAMERA

EYE	TV CAMERA
Active, easily stimulated by by natural movement	Static, must use staged movement that has a purpose, to manipulate eye of viewer
Wide field of view; many objects to focus on; nonselective	Narrow field of view, natural emphasis is on selected objects located in center of screen, promotes feeling of intimacy
Peripheral vision makes objects appear closer together than they are	Tunnelvision creates exaggeration of space between objects
Natural depth of field	Two-dimensional images with limited depth of field, must simulate environment and use angles to create a third dimension
Sees detail, aware of subtle differences	Lacks resolution, generalization of detail, unaware of subtle differences
Extensive contrast range* (10,000-1), detailed picture information within contrast range is easily identified	Limited contrast range (30-1), detailed picture information particularly in dark areas, is lost

*"Contrast range" equals the range between the darkest and
  lightest information as perceived in a given scene.

CHECKING THE LOCATION

Understanding field of view, aspect ratio, simulation, spatial relationships, contrast ratio, and how they effect the environment for TV production, you can now proceed to checking the location, better equipped to evaluate your needs for the shoot.

Most producers use a location checklist for shoots, as well as an equipment inventory sheet (both are included at the end of this chapter). These two sheets are to be used by the home video producer when going out to check a location. After going through the checklist, note what equipment and accessories will be needed on your inventory sheet.

At the location of the shoot, determine the power available for lighting requirements. Locate the appropriate power sources and determine which plugs belong to a particular circuit. The key is not how many outlets are in the room, but how many circuits are available. You can always check with a building electrician or the homeowner to find the circuit box. Note where natural light falls on the floor, coordinating with the approximate time of day that you will be shooting the real production. Natural light patterns and thus lighting requirements change as the time of day changes and the sun changes position.

Look carefully around the location. If it is a public place, are there going to be many people and a high noise level? It is important to examine the setting and the surrounding environment. Try to imagine and visualize the actions and the sequences that you have planned in your brainstorming outline. Are there colors or decorations that are problematic? Look at the composition and the setup of furniture. Will you have to switch things around or change angles to have better compositions and dimension? Use your checklists as you attempt to tie down the placement of audio and lights and commit to equipment needed on this location shoot. Take paper with you and sketch out floor plans, carefully noting everything of interest.

An excellent approach to dealing with the environment is to take your video camera with you to the location where (with a portable

TV) you can check it out to see how the scene is going to appear. This method will help pinpoint problem areas and allow you to begin to choose appropriate angles and shots. If you cannot take your portable video system with you, a Polaroid camera will at least give you a recorded image that you can use for reference. A visual record will also help you recall vital information once you leave the scene. Upon completion of the location checklist and filling out the inventory sheet you are ready to begin step four, which is one of the most exciting and fun steps.

LOCATION CHECKLIST FOR HVP "SHOOT"

(Remember, devise a floor plan. Locate <u>everything</u> on paper. If possible, use a Polaroid or video camera to record information.)

1. Note backgrounds at the different locations. Describe the locations, their color, contrast ratio, furnishings (whether they are detailed or simple), and what the spatial relationships are like between objects in the scene.

2. Determine the ambient noise problems at each location (e.g., many people in a crowd, street traffic, music) for appropriate mike selection and placement. Draw the placement on your floor plan.

3. Locate available AC power supply. Don't overload circuits; one normal circuit can handle <u>no more</u> that <u>15 amps</u> or about 1500 watts. Bring 3-prong adaptors and AC heavy-duty extension cords.

4. Determine quality and amount of available (natural or artificial) light at each location and determine angle of sun at hour approximating time of shoot. Look for shadow problems. Rough out the placement of your light fixtures on your floor plan.

5. Determine if crowd control will be necessary. You may need to have someone direct "traffic" around the shooting area.

6. Determine if auto traffic will be a problem. Maybe a traffic controller will be necessary.

7. Find a suitable (and secure) spot to unload and/or store equipment.

8. Select a "safe" area to leave equipment if extension cable is to be used. Arrange to leave someone with the equipment.

9. Make sure the crew and talent have transportation to and from the "location."

10. Identify any parking problems for vehicles carrying gear/talent/crew. Bring enough money to cover the expense.

11. Complete beforehand any details necessary to secure service of individuals (talent) belonging to a different organization (e.g., party entertainment).

12. Select suitable location for meals for talent and crew. Decide how meals will be served. Plan for proper trash disposal.

13. Double check arrival schedules of all talent at locations.

14. Predetermine who will provide location access. Contact person(s) authorized to provide you and crew access to the location(s).

15. Clear any security problems in advance.

16. Fill out your equipment inventory sheet based on what you see at the location (even though it may be revised later-- get a first impression of your needs).

Checked out by: _____ Location: _____

Date: _____ Program: _____

Time: _____

EQUIPMENT INVENTORY

TRANSPORTATION	OUT	IN
Vehicle		
Dollies		
Equipment pads		
Gas		
Parking money/permits		
PAPERWORK		
Release forms		
Script/Shot sheet		
Floor plan		
Log sheets		
Labels for videotapes/ audiotapes		
Location access permits		
CAMERA EQUIPMENT		
Camera w/case		
Camera extension cables		
Lens...(wide-angle, close-up & zoom) w/cases		
AC extension cords		
Tripod w/dolly & fluid head		
Fully charged batteries		
VCR EQUIPMENT		
Videotape recorder w/necessary cables... include AC power cables		
Fully charged batteries		
AC adaptor		
AC extension cords		
AC four-gang		
Videotape		
Color bar test tape		
Color TV (battery operated) w/cables		
Equipment carrier carts		

LIGHTING	OUT	IN
Portable light kits w/accessories		
Soft lights		
Light meter to measure footcandles		
AC extension cords		
AC four-gang		
Extra lamps		
Gaffers tape		
Reflector boards		
Diffusers & gels		
AUDIO		
Microphones... (lavaliers, interview, shotgun)		
Mike batteries		
Audio extension cables		
Audio mixer w/extra batteries		
Headphones w/extension cables		
Audio tape recorder w/audio & extra batteries		
MISCELLANEOUS		
Proper accessories bag		
Tool kit		
Stopwatch		
Slate		
Dulling spray		
Headcleaner can w/proper cleaning swabs (not Q-tips)		
Adaptors		
Masking tape		
Extra gaffers tape "3-prong" AC adaptor plugs		

IV

PICTURING THE ACTION

"In making a storyboard, you must
compose shots so that they will be in the
proper 3 x 4 aspect ratio for the television
screen."

CHAPTER 4

PICTURING THE ACTION

In step 4, Picturing the Action, you are going to begin working up a visual interpretation of your ideas. In this step you take your brainstorming outline and your understanding of the location and determine what's going to happen visually in each sequence throughout your program. What we are describing is "storyboarding," the visual treatment of shots and sequences. When we refer to a sequence, we are describing a connected or flowing series of shots at one location. Storyboarding is a time when you sit down and carefully plan these sequences, their shots, the blocking, the transitions, the graphics, and how it all should look in relation to each other. Chapter 5 will complete the visualization process by discussing how to make the shooting script and tie the storyboard to an actual shot sheet.

On some of your video pieces, picturing the action may be a step that takes a short amount of time. If you are covering an unfamiliar spontaneous event, such as a vacation, you will probably not be able to carefully design the shots in each sequence. Even the sequences may be uncertain. In this case, you will have to concentrate on the major subjects and the types of interviews you want to capture. Do a minimum storyboard if you can, and see Hints for Shooting Without a Script at the end of Chapter 5.

In order to picture the action you must be aware of several important concepts:

1) The importance of storyboarding <u>particularly if you are not using postproduction editing and are editing in-camera as you go</u> and the elements that make a storyboard.

2) The need for blocking and visual design for the screen.

3) The use of basic, transitional, and specialty shots; their sizes and uses.

4) The use of graphics.

THE STORYBOARD

Based on your time, interest, and the complexity of the event you are preplanning, you may choose to use a complete shot-by-shot storyboard or a generalized sequential one. We recommend, at the very least, a storyboard by sequence as it is a visual experience which encourages you to develop your sense of imagery and continuity.

Preplanning your visuals is very creative. Don't be afraid to try storyboarding. It is particularly important for taping events like a wedding, an important party, or even a "day in the life of your family." It ensures that you will end up with more than a big talking face or a series of unrelated shots. In a storyboard, you map out the important elements. You analyze the sequences, what is going to be happening in each, and the basic shots you will need to get.

Before you storyboard, <u>decide if you are going to edit after the shoot is over (in postproduction) or if you are going to edit in-camera while taping</u>. Editing is the electronic joining together of different video shots, eliminating breakup of picture between tape starts and stops. If you edit in postproduction at an editing house (names/addresses listed in phone book) you'll find it simple, moderately priced (about $15/hour without operator), and you can create a very finished-looking product. This type of editing is accomplished by using two VCRs and an automatic editing controller. In this way you build a new tape from existing field footage after the shoot and can manipulate sequences and shots in any order you desire. Therefore, the order of your storyboard can be more flexible. Several manufacturers have introduced simple home video editing systems (two VCRs and a controller) which will also accept other accessories such as a titling unit. As more home editors are introduced and prices come down, eventually the serious home video maker producing regularly will find it essential to his art, and more cost-effective as well, to purchase his own editing system.

While editing between two VCRs allows you to manipulate sequences in time and space, in-camera editing does not. If you are editing in-camera you use only the VCR during the shoot, and cannot manipulate the order of the video. You must therefore edit as you go, laying down sequences and shots chronologically on your tape while you are shooting. This requires a very organized storyboard, and is why preplanning is so important.

For those of you doing in-camera editing (working without the use of postproduction editing), it is very important for your storyboard to be as carefully planned as possible, so you will be able to shoot each sequence in the order it needs to be shown. In Chapter 5, when you actually make up a shot sheet, you will order your shoot including all the specialty shots from your storyboard (reaction shots, establishing shots, cutaways, etc.) that will add drama, interest, and vitality to each sequence.

What we are doing with a storyboard is beginning to use a TV screen's 3x4 aspect ratio and a paper and pencil to begin visualizing how one shot leads to another to build a sequence and make a completed tape. You can make your storyboard as simple or as complicated as you wish. Filling in the storyboard does not require that a person be able to draw. Make stick figures for people, and use a few words under each screen to explain how the picture will look. Let us say you are planning a 10-minute program for a birthday party. Chances are that a 10-minute tape might contain six to seven locations. Each sequence typically will be made up of two or three shots. Go out to the graphic supply store and buy yourself a pad of paper and a large piece of cardboard. On the cardboard you draw a series of television screens replicating TV's 3x4 aspect ratio. That aspect ratio is the reality in television. Anything we plan to do with television must be designed and composed for the 3x4 aspect ratio. Draw these television screens in pencil, take an exacto knife and cut the screens out, pull the piece of cardboard away and you now have a template of TV screens. Put the template over a piece of white paper and with a felt marker or pen, draw in your TV screens. Pull the template away and you have a sheet filled with empty television screens. Now you can begin to diagram, and design quickly and effectively your picnic, wedding, family gathering, or important family interview. See the sample storyboard sheet provided at the end of this chapter.

BLOCKING AND VISUAL DESIGN

There are many things to consider as you draw your visuals on a storyboard. Remember, television has a very limited field of view--only 45°. You must consciously compose shots so that they will appear properly in the 3x4 aspect ratio of the television screen. As stated in Chapter 3, the eye sees a very wide horizon (almost 180°) and is limited vertically, what you see with the naked eye is not what you will see through the viewfinder of your camera, or on your TV. To deal with this transition and to create a 3-dimensional image from a 2-dimensional screen, you must consider the following rules for good blocking and visual design:

1) Important information must be kept within the center of the screen.

2) The talent and objects on the TV screen, if spaced properly, provide a successful suggestion of the third dimension--DEPTH. Eliminate or move objects that cause the eye to read horizontally. Put objects in front of and in back of center action to create this illusion of depth.

3) The space between objects and/or talent on the horizon in the TV picture appears exaggerated. Block objects closer to talent and block talent at angles to each other using an inverted "L" shape or "V" shape configuration. Angular configurations allow people to be closer to each other than normal and still maintain a comfortable social distance. Identify and use appropriate safety distances for particular talent and crew. Positioning talent too close to each other, or crew too close to talent can inhibit/limit natural conversation.

Distancing between talent can also be used to create moods:

SUBJECT PLACEMENT	EFFECT
Subjects placed close to each other (1 to 2 feet)	Suggests intimacy, intensity
Subjects placed comfortably from each other (3 to 4 feet)	Suggests friendship, discussion, interaction
Subjects placed with some distance from each other (5 to 10 feet)	Suggests indifference, coldness, anger, hostility

SUBJECT PLACEMENT/EFFECT

1-2 ft.
Intimate

3-4 ft.
Friendly

5-10 ft.
Coldness

BLOCKING

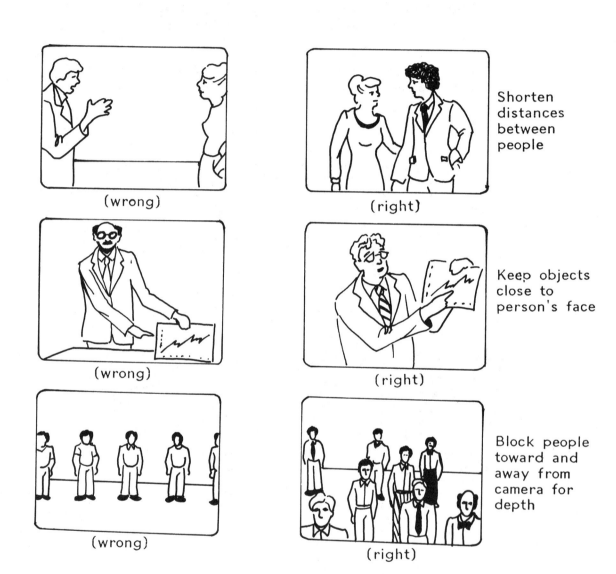

(wrong)   (right)   Shorten distances between people

(wrong)   (right)   Keep objects close to person's face

(wrong)   (right)   Block people toward and away from camera for depth

4) Broad action and/or short movements on the TV screen can appear to take longer than usual to complete. Plan to shorten the physical distance and time span between movements. This is done by taping the action as it begins, and then again as it is being completed (e.g., eating something delicious like birthday cake could be shot as cake is being cut and served, with the next shot showing someone eating and looking satisfied).

5) Does your shot move or is it stationary? Movement must be motivated. There also has to be a reason for the talent or subject to move. Both talent movement and camera composition are far more interesting toward or away from the camera, than to the left or right of it. Use depth rather than the horizon for picture composition. Consider the objects in front of and behind the subject, their importance, and the range of movement of your talent. Can you get it all in one shot with your lens, or do you need two shots? If many zooms are required, space multiple talent or objects equidistant from the camera in a semicircle. This enables you to hold focus as your camera moves from one person or object to another.

6) Keep environments simple, and clean. A suggestion of what is really there is sufficient for the viewer to feel comfortable with the location. A key to moving objects/people successfully within an environment is understanding that backgrounds for video are simulated, rather than duplicated. On location, it is commonplace that the existing environment is cluttered, and if not simplified, the detail will overwhelm the main subject on the screen.

7)   Always consider angle and elevation of the camera and its operator in relationship to the talent.

USE	EFFECT
High angle of camera looking down on subject	Suggests weakness, vulnerability, disregard
Normal angle of camera slightly lower than subject	Suggests peer status, equality to viewer, accessibility
Low angle of camera, looking up at subject	Suggests strength, respect, dominance, power

8)   Essential to good talent performance when maximum viewer attention is needed, is the use of eye contact. Without it, the viewer can lose the intensity of the talent's content and delivery. Eye contact is achieved by directing the talent to look into the lens of the camera and establish visual contact with the lens and thus the viewer. Often it must be staged, particularly on location shoots with inexperienced talent. Have the interviewer stand next to the camera with his eyes level at the lens and looking supportively at the talent, encouraging eye contact; or shoot over the interviewer's shoulder, having the camera directly facing the person talking.

Understanding the above visual relationships and blocking rules is essential to creating meaningful visuals with the proper composition for the television screen. These rules for good television pictures, when combined with a working knowledge of "shots"-- their sizes and uses--will enable you to design a storyboard that will accurately and effectively display an outline of the visual needs of your program.

BASIC SHOTS

In order to become familiar with a variety of camera shots, try viewing television with the sound off. Observe what kind of camera shots are chosen in relationship to the subject and action. Watch how the shots change size. Visual emphasis on the subject or background is often determined by the shot's size. You will observe that there are four basic shots in television. They are: wide shot, medium shot, close-up, and extreme close-up. (See illustration--page 69.)

1) Wide Shot ("Long Shot" or "Establishing Shot")

 * For viewer orientation--a wide field of view.

 * Usually an opening shot to root the audience by establishing location and revealing surroundings.

 * Used to show signage of a location.

 * Used to cover broad action involving several people in a large area.

2) Medium Shot ("Waist Shot," "Bust Shot," "Shoulder Shot")

 * TV's most popular shot, used when shooting one to three people from the waist up. Commercial TV usually changes shot size from a wide shot to a medium shot.

 * Standard shot for interviews. Reveals background and location while focusing attention on 1, 2, or 3 people at a comfortable conversational distance.

 * Good for covering short action.

3) <u>Close-up Shot</u> ("Tight Shot" or "Head Shot")

* An emphasis shot, focusing viewer's attention on a specific detail (e.g., contents of a letter) or person (e.g., important speech).

* A shot with impact. Demands viewer concentration on particular information/subject.

* Subtle movement works best with the close-up. Broad movement is hard to contain in the picture frame. Close-ups are used with broad action, sparingly, and only for dramatic effect.

4) <u>Extreme Close-up</u> ("Hot Shot")--USE SPARINGLY

* Very dramatic shot with visual excitement. Used for emotional moments. Hard for a viewer to look at for a long time.

* An intimate shot. Can detail eyes, nose, and mouth (sacrifice forehead for chin space).

* Can also detail hand movements on a watch face, keys on a typewriter, etc., for visual impact.

* After using this shot for dramatic impact, director usually shifts size and angle for the next shot of the subject.

BASIC SHOTS IN TELEVISION

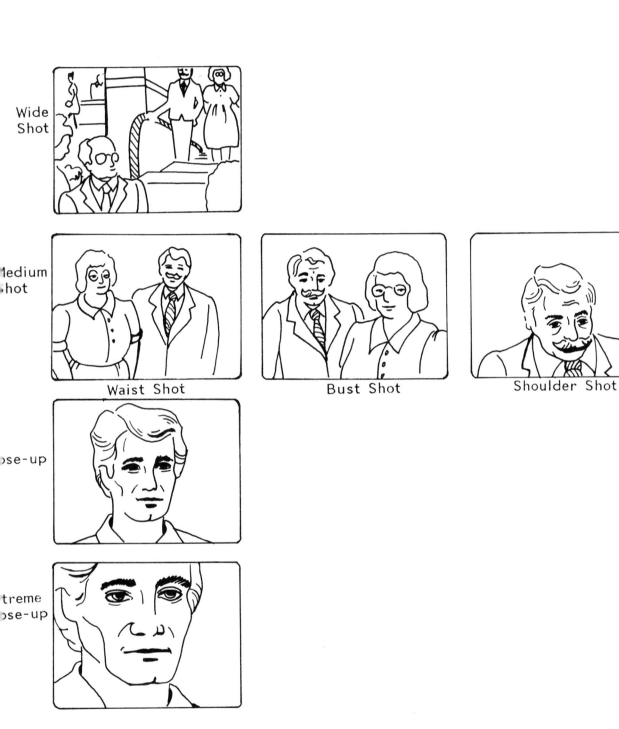

Wide Shot

Medium Shot

Waist Shot

Bust Shot

Shoulder Shot

Close-up

Extreme Close-up

CHANGING SHOT SIZE

While the zoom lens can move you automatically through these basic shot positions, there are times when you will be stopping and starting your tape and changing shot sizes. The basic rules regarding changes in shot size are:

1) Changes in shot size usually occur progressively. That is, you move from a wide shot to a medium shot, a bust shot to a shoulder shot to a close-up. Extreme changes in shot size (e.g., from a medium shot to an extreme close-up) are visually jarring to the viewer and should be used only for impact, like getting attention in an opening by going from a wide establishing shot to a shoulder shot of the talent speaking.

2) When not using a zoom lens, changes in shot size on the same subject should always be accompanied by a change in camera angle. If you stop and start the camera, moving from a medium shot to a close-up of the subject without changing the angle, you will get a jump cut (i.e., one shot will seem to "jump" or "pop" to the next). A jump cut is distracting to viewers and should be avoided. If you are in-camera editing, and want to shorten a long interview answer to the first question, before you ask the next question, back up the tape, and change the size and the angle of the shot.

During the shooting of an event then, you will not only be concerned with use of the basic four shots to cover the content, but with the length of those shots as well. Certainly you will not want to cover a 3-hour event by shooting 3 hours of tape, especially if you are limited to in-camera editing. No director ever really knows in advance how long a particular interview is going to be. Still you must attempt to plan the sequence length. To do that, you will have to be concerned with condensing time and space. This means, if using in-camera editing, making the decision that you've gotten what you need and it is time to stop the camera. Reposition the camera, changing the size and angle of the next shot. In addition, during storyboarding, you should plan to use specialty and transitional shots (even more necessary with in-camera editing). These shots help shorten the sequence as well as provide a smooth connective to the next sequence.

TRANSITIONAL SHOTS

The basic transitional shots which help us move smoothly from one sequence to another are:

1) Establishing shot--a cover, orientation, or identification shot of the new sequence location. Usually one shot held a few seconds with an immediate cut to an intimate shot of the new sequence.

2) Fade-up or down--an effect, consisting of going from black to picture at the beginning of a scene, and from picture to black at the end. Sometimes used between sequences to simulate a passage of time. A fade may be done by manual control of the lens aperture at the beginning and/or end of a particular shot.

3) Pan--a left or right horizontal movement of the camera used as a quick transition between somewhat related sequences. A quick "swish" pan may be used for bridging unrelated scenes, giving the feeling of movement and/or action between space and/or time.

4) Defocus--a manual adjustment of the lens focus, taking it out of range, blurring the picture, used when changing locations and refocusing on the new shot.

Don't plan a transition shot that requires your viewers to both listen to a new audio narration or description, and also watch a lot of new video action. It becomes too confusing for your viewer, and it makes it difficult for him to focus in on the new sequence. When you plan a transitional shot, either the audio or the video must be very passive, and not require a lot of

71

attention, so that the viewer can concentrate on the active portion.

SPECIALTY SHOTS

Basic specialty shots allow you to shorten a sequence. They also add interest, depth, and drama to any sequence. The specialty shots are:

1) Reaction shot--A single shot, showing a reaction or opposite point of view from the previous shot: every action has a reaction. A reaction shot can be catching the facial expression of those people surrounding an action. For example, when covering your child's soccer game, include a shot of the coach's face during an exciting play. Not only will that reaction shot add drama to the game, but it allows you to shorten the whole game. You can leave an intense play, show the coach's reaction, and come back to another sequence later on in the game--perhaps a wide shot of the team running down the field. Reaction shots are also important in interviews to remind viewers that "someone" is receiving the information. If you stop your camera the audio is also interrupted. Where continuous audio is needed, show reactions using a pan shot.

2) Cutaway--A shot or a series of shots in a sequence, used to illustrate an example of what is being discussed. In an interview if someone is talking about an object or person, you could cut to a shot of that object or person to add clarity and dimension to the interview. For instance, if you are on location, reviewing a 10-minute interview with Grandma about her garden, and after 3 minutes decide that's plenty (audio and video)--you could cue up the tape at 3 minutes, in-camera edit a cutaway of the garden, and this way shorten the interview by 7 minutes and be ready to establish the next sequence. Often if the cutaway is close to the person talking, the camera can pan directly

to that subject, hold for a moment, and pan back to the person. Plan your interviews, if possible, in locations where the cutaways exist.

GRAPHICS

Graphics, such as titles and credits, are the last element that must be considered, planned into the shoot, and noted on your storyboard. You may want to give dates, title different sequences, and list crew members. You will need time before the shoot to design and make your own graphics. If you are not going to shoot graphics at the time of the event be sure to leave space at the beginning of the tape, so they can be included in postproduction.

TV graphics must be tailored to the television screen's 3x4 aspect ratio. The size of the graphic card will usually be 11x14, or 15x20 inches. The local art supply store can provide stiff matte board. The graphic card must be heavy enough to lay flat. The finish must be dull. Try to maintain moderate contrast between the various elements of the graphic card. Avoid a white background--it is too reflective. A light TV blue or middle gray cardboard is better.

When preparing graphic cards, divide the card into two primary areas--the "safe information" area and the "bleed" area. (See illustration on page 75.)

The most important part of the graphic card is the <u>safe information area</u>. Important information must be placed within this safe area on the graphic card to ensure proper display on any or all TV screens. All television sets do not display information on the screen exactly alike. Important information must not be allowed to extend to the edge of the TV screen. The safe information area is usually 80% of the width and 80% of the height of the screen from the center of the card.

The bleed area is the imaginary border (usually two inches in
from edge of card), around the safe information area. It is the
same color as the background of the safe information area. If
you find you are constantly generating a great many graphics, it
might help to cut out a mask (template) of the safe area and use
it to prepare invisible margins on additional cards. Be careful
that you don't leave tracing marks.

Since TV is a low resolution (detail) medium--so artwork must be
simple, uncomplicated, and always readable. Keep the lettering
simple and bold. Stay away from fancy types that may be
difficult for TV to read. This can be even more critical if you
plan to key or superimpose your graphics over an existing
background (like using Sony's HVS 2000 video camera selector).
Try choosing a typeface like Helvetica Medium or Franklin Gothic
so that the information is easily readable. They are available in
acetate "stick-ons" at stationary and artist supply stores.

Letters for graphic cards should be at least one-half inch in
height (never less than one-tenth the height of the screen area).
Try to maintain approximately one inch of space between the
lines. Generally, place no more than three full lines of
information on the screen at any one time. Avoid more than ten
words on the screen at any one time.

Record the shot of the graphic card long enough for a viewer to
get the information. Usually, if you can read the information
twice, without rushing, it has been up long enough. Leave the
graphic on longer if the information is of a precise or technical
nature.

Graphics must have good lighting. You can avoid a distracting
glare by placing illumination at $45°$ angles to the graphic card.

PREPARING GRAPHIC CARDS

GRAPHIC CARD

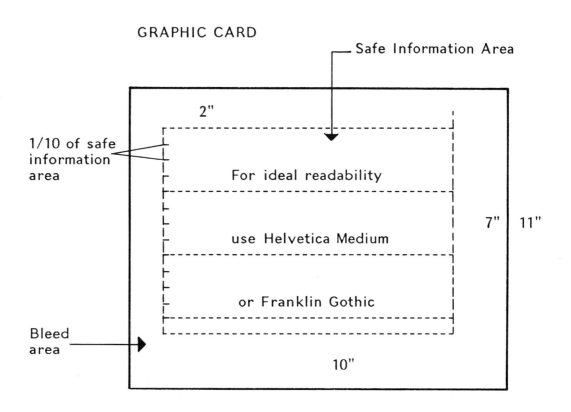

There are cameras available now that offer limited titling features, much like simple character generators. If your camera has a titling feature, be sure to include titles, dates, names, introductions, and credits during the shoot. These planned graphics will make your program look more professional. More sophisticated character generators are available at postproduction facilities. A character generator is approximately the size of a portable typewriter and electronically processes the letters selected at a keyboard. Basic features include:

* At least 16 pages (think of a page as a graphic card) that can be placed into a memory bank and be recalled at will.

* A variety of type faces and styles that will boldly stand out on TV. (Check, however, to make sure typeface is of adequate height for readability.)

* An ability to internally generate colored matte backgrounds for the letters to appear over.

* An ability to have lines either crawl across the screen (right or left), or up and down the screen.

* An edging capability to add legibility to letters.

* An ability to place graphic information over a prerecorded videotape.

There are also a whole variety of existing graphics in the environment (such as signs, drawings, photographs, and print materials) that you should consider. If you are doing a family picnic, which is happening in a park, you may want to begin your tape titled with a shot of the park sign as you enter. You may want to start your birthday tape with a close-up of the cake, saying "Happy Birthday Tom," which will essentially act as a title to the whole tape that is going to occur. If you are doing an interview with your grandmother and grandfather, you may want to start on their wedding picture on their dresser, zoom out, and pan over to reveal them sitting on a couch and begin their interview.

Consider integrating your home collection of slides, photographs, and movies into the finished program. Slides and photographs can easily be recorded by your television camera (project slides on a small area 11x14 inches to shoot at maximum intensity, or use Sony's VCR-4 telecine adaptor). Remember, television does not resolve detail well, so choose slides and photographs that are simple and have the major subject information in the middle of the frame. Let the information on the photos and slides bleed to the edges of your TV camera; otherwise, borders on the TV screen will be visible and distracting.

Recording home movies on videotape, however, is more involved. Home movies play back at 24 frames a second; video records at 30 frames a second. If you record through your TV camera off a screen you will pick up a flicker throughout the tape. To avoid this flicker, you can buy a home TV/film chain which corrects for the speed differences. If you do not have a lot of movies to convert, we suggest having your film inexpensively transferred to tape (at a place like Fotomat). By using the newly created home movie tapes with your other tapes, you've retrieved portions of your family history to use in the final program.

As you can see, there is more than just sketching in making the storyboard. It involves consideration of blocking and visual design, shots, and graphics. It is a good opportunity to enjoy with your family or friends the fun of picturing the action and committing to a game plan for your shoot. Remember, there will always be spontaneous shots in a sequence that will be irresistible and those you will want to include. Having a plan is what keeps you calm and focused during the shoot. It allows you to be choosy about adding that something extra.

STORYBOARD

Video:

Shot:
Description, Movement,
Cues

Audio:
Dialogue, Cues,
Instruction

V

MAKING THE SHOOTING SCRIPT

"You must make an outline of the shots
and sequences that cover the essence of
what you want to record."

CHAPTER 5

MAKING THE SHOOTING SCRIPT

We will become even more prepared for the shoot as we interpret the storyboard into a script and/or shot sheet. We will also consider composition, movement, and depth of field of our camera, which will translate our script into a finished program.

SCRIPTING

A script, like the storyboard, is simply a game plan. The script is an extension of the storyboard. There are full scripts and partial scripts. A full script is a word-for-word rendition of everything that is going to happen. All of the spoken material is on one side of the page (normally the right side) and all of the corresponding shots (production cues) are on the left side. The full script ties the camera shots to specific word cues. Unless you are videographing a play, full scripts are extremely difficult when using nonprofessional talent. It is not realistic to expect people in home video who are not actors to memorize a full script of dialogue and then perform naturally and effectively in front of the camera.

In most of the productions you will be doing on home video, do not tie people down to a word-for-word rendition of what is going to happen. What you need is a shooting plan. You want to allow your home talent to be somewhat spontaneous and natural. You need an outline of the shots and sequences that cover the essence of what you want to record.

RUNDOWN SHEET

In Making the Shooting Script, we recommend the use of a "rundown" sheet which utilizes the capabilities of home talent and home scriptwriters. A rundown sheet ties the camera shot to a major subject (specific content) and/or major action (talent movement). On your storyboard you should have already decided on your major subjects and actions, and should have also illustrated the basic shot sizes. As you move from storyboarding to scripting you translate those visuals, illustrated in your storyboard, to specific shot directives. You mark those commands in abbreviated form on the left side of your rundown sheet and tie them to the specific content (subject) or the talent movement (action), noted on the right side.

By making a rundown sheet, you are developing a quick reference guide to refer to during the heat of the shoot. As things happen fast and furious on location, you won't have time to read paragraphs. Rather, you will need instant cues to keep you on target with what you need to accomplish. If for some reason these cues do not suffice, you can always stop between sequences and consult your storyboard, to refresh yourself of the total blocking and visual concept you had in mind.

The following example is a section of a rundown sheet:

Symbols for Shots: WS = Wide Shot   SS = Shoulder Shot
                     MS = Medium Shot   CU = Close-up
                     BS = Bust Shot   ZI = Zoom-in

VIDEO	SUBJECTS/ACTION
Leave 5 sec. black on tape; fade up to f/5.6 ------------------------------ INTRODUCTION (1) WS Mom (in kitchen ZI - BS Mom	(event, date) (why special)
(2) MS Mom (PAN rt.)	WALKS to birthday cake
(3) BS Mom (at counter)	INTERVIEW about birthday child
(4) CU Mom's hands & cake	Mom places candles on cake
(5) WS Group at table w/ b-day child (rt) Move in MS b-day child & Mom	Mom ENTERS (lft) with cake, (SINGING) Mom puts down cake in front of b-day child

SHOT SHEET

Very often, after the rundown sheet is prepared, a director will also prepare a shot sheet. The shot sheet is a chronological list of the shots you want to get, taken from your rundown sheet. During rehearsal and the shoot, the director uses the rundown sheet as his shooting guide. The cameraperson uses the shot sheet as his guide. If you are both director and cameraperson, then you might want to consider listing your shots in order on a small piece of paper and taping it to the side of your camera as a continual reminder of your next shot(s).

The rundown sheet and particularly the shot sheet can be a tremendous help when you are out there in the middle of the action and all of a sudden people are running around, kids are screaming and pulling on your cables, and you are trying to figure out what kinds of shots you should be going after!

CAMERAWORK

With the rundown and shot sheets complete, you can move onto location confident. When you begin the shoot, you will be able to concentrate on polishing the action--that is, shooting with emphasis on good camerawork (focus, zooms, composition, and movement)--rather than capturing the action--where concerns are more primitive (e.g., "What size shot should I be on to get that action?").

Good camerawork takes time to develop. As a cameraperson you must first know your camera thoroughly. You should take the time to study your operator's manual and make sure you understand how to set your camera up for optimum picture quality. As you log shooting hours, you need to analyze your shots and composition. Practice when and how to zoom and hold focus--and when and how to physically move with the camera. As time goes on, you will develop the ability to go on location and be able to move through your shot sheet with your work looking better and better.

Complete rundown and shot sheets allow you the time during the shoot to concentrate on the quality of your camerawork. Knowing your camera, practicing, and applying the following rules of composition, movement, and depth of field will help you to use your camera to its best advantage, and produce good video.

COMPOSITION

Good composition suggests a picture that looks balanced, and directs audience attention to the important elements in a shot. Use the following hints to achieve good composition:

* To introduce the feeling of <u>depth</u> to a 2-dimensional TV screen, shoot using creative angles with objects in the foreground as well as the background.

* Have talent move "toward" and "away from" the camera to lend interest and impact to the picture.

* Use the over-the-shoulder shot when two or more people are communicating with each other, to suggest relationships. This shot introduces depth into the shot. This is a popular setup for interviews.

* Allow for a proper amount of "headroom" (usually 10% of the picture height). Too little looks cramped, and too much can appear bottom heavy, making talent look unimportant. On extreme close-ups sacrifice the forehead and allow more room for the chin.

* Allow for a proper amount of "lead space" when shooting profiles (usually no more than 20% of the picture width). Arrange the shot with more space in front of the talent's profile and less space behind. The camera must also anticipate and allow free space in the direction of talent movement.

* Avoid large areas of the TV screen appearing empty--
especially in the center of the picture. Empty space in the
picture's center draws attention away from the main
subject(s). Change blocking and camera angles to gain
better perspective.

* Usually subjects facing the camera should be centered on the
screen for balance. Try to put the focus of the shot in the
center of the screen.

* A subject in profile, i.e., not facing the camera, should be
off-centered on the screen with the proper amount of lead
space in front.

* Watch out for extreme differences in height between talent.
Compensate by equalizing height--having talent sit rather
than stand.

MOVEMENT

If the viewer is going to be able to concentrate on the content
being delivered, movement of the subject, camera, and lens must
be motivated and smooth. Use the following hints to achieve
proper movement.

* Only move the camera to follow action, to give emphasis, or
to reveal something to the viewer. Avoid confused movement
that has no reason or motivation. It becomes obvious and
distracts the viewer from the program.

* Subject movement toward and away from the camera creates
the illusion of depth, adds dimension and impact.

* The zoom lens is moved (zoomed) in to provide emphasis and
lend drama to subject's word, action, or presence. It is
moved (zoomed) out to reveal more of the subject and
environment, to cover a broad action, or to root the viewer

visually. A lens is never moved (zoomed) on a stationary subject for a change of pace unless there is a change of pace in the subject's content or emotion. Zooms do not happen to avoid boredom on the screen. Lens movement must be motivated. Once a zoom-in is effected, there is a commitment. Don't zoom in and out, in and out, or viewer confusion will result.

* Learn how to shift, and readjust camera focus as subject-to-camera distances change during a continuous shot.

* The camera is usually mounted on a quality tripod with a fluid head to cover stationary subjects or talent. The moves of a camera on a tripod consist of zooming in and out, panning left or right, tilting up and down. Very often these moves are combined, occurring simultaneously, and a good cameraperson has to practice to be smooth and hold focus. (Typical examples are: zooming in and tilting up to hold headroom on a subject. Zooming out and tilting down to avoid too much headroom above the subject. Panning to something lower or higher than the eye level of talent usually requires a simultaneous tilt as well. Sometimes the shot move may require a pan, tilt, and zoom all at once.) Remember, skillful and smooth camerawork takes time and practice.

* The camera usually physically moves to cover moving subjects, or action. Hand-held and shouldered (often with a body-pod for extra stability), camera moves consist of "trucking" left or right and "dollying" in and out (trucking and dollying are old studio terms and could be changed to command terms you feel more comfortable with, like simply "move left or right" and "move in or out"). For greater body stability when using your camera off its tripod the body should be positioned with: 1) elbow locked-in above the hip; 2) side of face against camera; 3) feet apart (golf stance) with toes out; 4) gliding forward, shifting weight from the stationary leg to the toe of the other leg coming down; 5) for maximum stability during the move, weight is always placed first on the toe, never the heel. (See illustration on page 90.)

Keep feet apart
with toes out

Glide forward
shifting weight to toe

* For good, smooth moving shots (on a tripod or physically moving), it is very important that you, the cameraperson, during rehearsal, first find the end of the shot. Focus on it. See what size and position it's going to be, and then move the camera back to the beginning of that shot. That way when you do the shot, you'll know very specifically where you're going and when to stop. If you don't know where you're going, then midway through the shot it shows in the camerawork, and the smooth movement suffers as you try to guess at what point to stop the camera.

* Generally, physical movement with the camera gives you a more intimate and closer feeling when covering action or interaction. A moving camera on a stationary subject could be very distracting, although two subjects interacting could work fine with a camera moving back and forth. Zooming in and out with camera lens, while your camera is stationary, gives the viewer a cooler, more detached type of feel on the screen. Zooms are more standard, but more difficult to hold in focus if there is a lot of subject movement toward and away from the camera.

* Usually, for physical movement or for broad action, your lens should be on a wide-angle shot. Camera shake is less visible on a wide-angle shot. A wide angle enlarges or exaggerates perspective, and also offers an intimate, dramatic shot when you physically move in for a close-up shot. The lens in a wide-angle position has its greatest depth of field, which allows your camera to move around with minimum focusing problems.

DEPTH OF FIELD

Once a person or object is in focus, all "information" in front of and behind the object which is also in focus, is the "depth of field." It is determined either by f/stop, the size of the shot, and/or subject-to-camera distance. Depth of field can be used very creatively. Use the following hints to best decide how depth of field can aid your shot:

* A high f/stop (lens closed down), a wide-angle shot (lens zoomed out), and a short subject-to-camera distance, all increase the depth of field of a shot, enhancing foreground and background detail.

* A low f/stop (lens opened up), a close-up shot (lens zoomed in), and a long subject-to-camera distance, all decrease the depth of field of a shot causing distracting foregrounds and background to blur out.

Having analyzed the use of your camera, and made your shooting script (rundown sheet and/or shot sheet), you should begin to assign crew roles. By now you know what the event will look like, have completed your location checkout, and put together the types of shots and sequences you want to achieve. It is important to choose crew members from family and friends who you feel can perform the best job for you. If you do bring together a capable crew--separate people for director, cameraperson, and audio--then it is important that you find an efficient way to communicate with them. When you are on location shooting, it is best to communicate using hand gestures and/or minimal terms so that all crew members immediately know what each person is talking about. This is important to working as a team and being able to get what you need during the shoot. This signal system must be one that you all agree upon and understand, so that when things start happening and get very exciting, you can communicate quickly and act upon it. Hand signals can be as simple as "zoom in," "zoom out" (arm and fist moving in and out), or "move left," "move right" (thumb and open palm moving left or right). We think one of the biggest problems of location work and one of the biggest challenges to your crew is being able to see something happen, an action take place that was not planned for, and being able to react quickly and capture it.

Once the crew is organized, your preplanning is almost complete. Now it is time to gather your crew and your equipment and get ready for the big event. You are almost ready to experience the exhilaration and excitement of the actual shoot. But first, there is one more step. In Chapter 6 we discuss setting up the shoot.

CAMERA SHOT LIST

Shot sheets are suitable for use when camera shots are planned in advance. List individual camera shots sequentially from beginning to end so cameraperson can automatically move from shot to shot.

Director:_____

Camera Person:_____

Date:_____

Time:_____

Location:_____

Program:_____

1. _____	11. _____
2. _____	12. _____
3. _____	13. _____
4. _____	14. _____
5. _____	15. _____
6. _____	16. _____
7. _____	17. _____
8. _____	18. _____
9. _____	19. _____
10. _____	20. _____

HINTS FOR SHOOTING WITHOUT A SCRIPT

When you arrive at each location.   STOP.
                                    LOOK.
                                    LISTEN.

* Think sequences. Try to plan several shots for each sequence.

* Continually evaluate if what you're going to shoot is need-to-know or nice-to-know. Remember you're looking for a beginning, middle, and end. You'll need to quickly develop a point of view about the content of the shoot.

* Try to begin each sequence with a cover shot. Shoot in the following order LS, MS, and CU. Remember, CUs are important for detail and impact. Wide shots cover the action. Watch your viewfinder for good composition.

* Try to listen to dialogue to better understand the visuals needed. Shoot objects, environments, subjects that provide additional information (details) to be used as cutaways and inserts. If in-camera editing: be calm, don't jump from shot to shot too much. The audio stops each time you stop the camera. Minimize cutaways and inserts. Pick up cutaways, inserts, and reaction shots during interviews by quick pans during the next question being asked.

* Cover unsuspected action on a wide shot. Use a wide lens and close subject-to-camera distance to maximize depth of field (focus).

* Change size of your shot and angle during questions of an interview or during pauses of the speaker.

* Remember shooting while moving the camera requires you know where you're going to end the shot in advance. If you start a move, take it to its finish. The tighter the size

of the shot, the more apparent camera shake will be during the move.

* Be careful of large props placed directly in front of, or behind talent, which may create visual barriers or appear to be "growing" out of the back of their head!

* When possible block talent at least 6 feet from a background wall so that shadows will drop and fall on the floor, rather than on wall above talent's shoulders.

* Be careful of bright sources (e.g., sunlight, windows, chrome, jewelry) which can wash out the picture or burn the tube of your camera. Remember if you can't relocate the action to get rid of a bad or distracting background, you can almost always move your camera.

* Be sure and do periodic audio/video playback checks to make sure all is working well. Have extra tape and batteries with you. Audio should be continually monitored with a headset.

VI

SETTING UP THE SHOOT

**"Plan to set up your equipment and lights
at least one hour before shooting time."**

CHAPTER 6

SETTING UP THE SHOOT

Setting up properly before the shoot is very important, because it will save you time during the taping. The more you can do before the event begins, the smoother and the more fun the taping will be. The more variables you properly attend to before the shoot begins, the better you will be able to focus on following your program plan (rundown sheet or shot sheet) without getting confused. Feeling prepared will make you better able to shoot those unexpected moments that become important to the event.

DAY BEFORE THE EVENT

The day before the event, there are several things you should do:

1) Review the inventory form and floor plan that you completed in the location checkout. The most important thing you do before you leave anywhere, or go anyplace, is to check your inventory list. It is not likely you will forget to take the big items, like cameras or tripods, but it is easy to forget an extension cable, light stand, or other small item. Another advantage in referring to your inventory sheet is to ensure you come back with everything that you took.

2) Gather the accessories and equipment required. You should have a bag where you can keep all your accessories: videotape, masking tape, labels, pen, batteries, cables, connectors, etc.

3) Make sure that all the equipment is working. Carefully check your connectors, cables, and adaptors. Make a test recording and play it back to be sure it all works.

4)   Make confirmation calls. You should confirm that the event will indeed take place, that the family or friends acting as crew or talent know what time to arrive, and that the special stars of the tape will be there. Be sure to confirm pickup or delivery times on any rentals (special lights/audio, props) as well as starting times of special segments at the event (such as a singing telegram at a birthday party). If the event is not being held in your home, call and confirm early access to the location for equipment setup.

DAY OF THE EVENT

The day of the event, plan to arrive at your location with your crew at least one hour before shooting time. Always set up the lights from your floor plan diagram before any of your other equipment. This takes the longest time. Use a talent stand-in to check the lighting and get it correct. Then set up your audio, camera, and the rest of the equipment for your first shot from your shot sheet (rundown script). View your TV to verify your lighting, audio, and camera setup. Tape all cables to the floor, so no one will trip. Do a test recording to make sure everything is operating and in the correct positions. Play back the tape and check for picture and sound quality.

Put extra equipment and accessories out of the way, but within easy access. It is very important that you are able to put your extra equipment someplace where it is safe, secure, and where you can get to it easily without having to have an official unlock a closet every time you want to get something.

The following checklist is designed to help you set up your shoot. While you may not need all the items listed for every event, many will apply.

Remember, all of these preparations should be done before the event begins, so you won't miss any of the action. The people and the event will not wait for you! But if you are properly prepared, you can move into the shoot feeling confident and excited. This checklist will serve as a handy reminder during the setup.

CHECKLIST FOR SETTING UP THE SHOOT

* ## Set up the lights

1. Position fixtures for stability (tape down the stand legs with gaffers [duct] tape or use sandbags on the legs for safety).

2. Check the height and angle of the lights. Barn doors should be moved to help control shadows. Pass a pencil in front of the light to determine where the beam falls. Another test of where your light falls is to turn off all lighting except the one light being tested. Look at the area illuminated.

3. Watch for distracting shadows.

4. Check for obvious light reflecting objects in the scene (such as chrome furniture or mirrors) and remove them if possible; or change your camera angle.

5. Tape down all lighting cables.

6. Label all extension cords with your name for easy identification when you "strike the set" (remove your equipment from the location).

* ## Set up the audio

1. Put batteries in all mikes that require them and check polarity ("+" and "-" contacts in right position).

2. Loop audio cables and secure to deck handle or carrying case strap. This relieves the stress of the cable on the VCR connector so it can't be pulled out of the input receptacle when tugged.

3. A hand-held mike should have enough cable so it can be used 6 to 12 inches from speaker's mouth and at chin level.

4. A shotgun mike should have enough cable so it can be used 12 to 15 feet from the subject.

5. Desk mikes should be placed approximately 2 feet from the speaker's mouth.

6. When placing a mike on a table, put mike on towel or foam cushion to absorb noise and vibration from the table top. If mike is going to be seen, use a mike stand with foam bottom.

7. If possible, when talent is stationary and you are taping at the same location for awhile, tape all audio cables down.

8. Remember, once the shoot begins sound must be monitored at all times by either you or a crew member, in order to detect unwanted sound, disconnections, or audio failures. Wear a headphone.

9. If you hear a buzz when hooking up an audio mixer, it could be a grounding problem. Rotate the AC plug in the wall socket to change the grounding polarity.

10. Never cross audio lines over power cables, as this also creates an audio buzz. If crossing lines cannot be avoided, put the two lines perpendicular to each other and secure the cross (+) with tape.

11. Drained batteries also produce an audio buzz, making it necessary to replace the batteries.

12. To set the sound level of a mixer, first set master "pot" (dial) to an average level of 6 or 7 on the volume control knob, then set each mike's volume control separately by turning down all mike pots except for mike being set.

13. Be sure to check audio levels on both deck and audio mixer. If you have a limiter on your deck, turn it off when setting audio levels (i.e., put in manual position), to get a true audio reading.

* Set up the camera

1. Set camera to correct color filter in relation to light source, and white balance the camera as per the

instructions on your camera's operation manual (if not done automatically).

2. Tape a shot sheet to the side of the camera for reference.

3. Change into comfortable, low-heeled, lightweight shoes that slide easily.

4. Practice moving shots (pans, zooms, etc.) by first locating and sizing the <u>ending</u> position of the desired shot. This allows you to always know where your camera is going from the beginning to the end of the shot.

5. Have the person responsible for the cables practice moving with the cameraperson during shots requiring motion. This will prevent anyone tripping over the cables or the cameraperson "caught short" because he did not have enough cable.

6. If the camera is to be hand-held, use a support person for the cameraperson. Positions used to help the cameraperson to steady a hand-held camera are:

   * Support person places his hands just under the shoulderblades of the cameraperson. This allows the cameraperson to lean back into the support person's hands.

   * When shooting from a low angle in a squat position, the support person puts one hand between the shoulderblades and the other hand low in the small of the back of the cameraperson. (See page 104.)

7. The support person and cameraperson must have a way to communicate in an abbreviated language decided upon before the shoot.

SUPPORT PERSON POSITIONS

* <u>Set up the VCR</u>

    1.   Set up VCR with camera, if camera is going to be stationary. If camera is going to move, use extension cable from VCR to camera and loop cable through the belt loop of the cameraperson to help keep the cable out of the way.

    2.   Make sure the VCR-to-camera cable is kept up off the ground to avoid anyone tripping, especially the cameraperson.

    3.   Label tape with title, date, number, and time shot.

    4.   Fast-forward and rewind entire tape before it is used to assure correct tape tension.

    5.   If shooting with batteries, check the battery level meter reading on VCR to make sure it shows a charge and is not reading in the red zone.

    6.   Have extra batteries handy.

    7.   Check all connections into the deck before shooting begins.

    8.   Check and tape together connectors on extension cables for video and audio equipment. Loop and tape cables to remove tension at point of connection.

    9.   Zero the counter before making test recordings and then log the test recording as you should all footage.

* <u>Use TV for verifying good audio, lighting & camera setup</u>

Check for:

    1.   Moderate contrast.

    2.   Simple composition free from busy detail.

    3.   No extra bright areas in corners of screen, or hot spots on furniture, or bright windows to draw attention

away from the subject and create burn problems for the camera.

4. Clear audio tones with no interference from cross wires or bad batteries.

* <u>Record an audio/video test</u>

    1. Tape for at least two minutes.

    2. Play back and check carefully.

* <u>Tape down all stationary cables with gaffers tape</u>

* <u>Brief crew members and talent</u>

    1. Review crew roles (based on the needs of this checklist).

    2. Review composition of shots and hand signals with cameraperson and crew.

    3. Crew should practice working together and any expected difficult maneuvers.

    4. If possible, role-play talent, reviewing important content. Encourage eye contact.

VII

TAPING THE EVENT

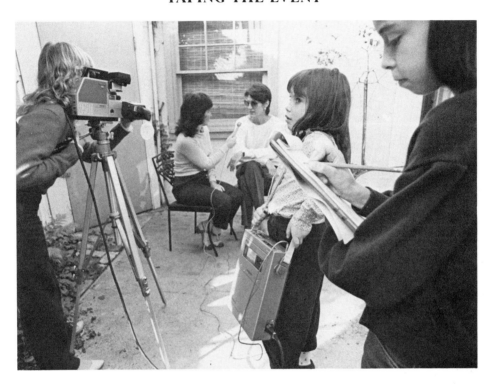

"You will be moving in and out of areas
with your camera, conducting on-the-spot
interviews and capturing the action."

CHAPTER 7

TAPING THE EVENT

In the first six steps, you've done a tremendous amount of planning and preparation. Now at last, the moment has arrived and you are ready to begin taping the production. For us, every time we go into a taping situation our blood begins to rush. Everything gets very exciting. It really is "Lights, Camera, Action!" For you, your family, and friends it will be the same. With the proper preplanning accomplished, taping the event will be a wonderful opportunity to move, in an organized fashion, through the coverage of the sequences you have developed.

The emphasis during taping the event is on the director. As the director, you must manage your crew, work with talent to tape good interviews, and make decisions that will result in good coverage of each sequence.

MANAGING YOUR CREW

Whether you have a crew of two or a crew of four, as the director you will be the organizing and calming force of the production. The director sets the pace. Your plan and guidance will prevent a chaotic situation. As the director, you must take the crew through a simple route of covering each sequence in your script, chronologically as the action occurs. You must continually communicate with your crew so everyone understands what they should be doing at all times. Communicating takes the most effort in the beginning, when you are not all accustomed to working together. With more experience, crewing becomes easier and fun as you learn to anticipate each other's needs. Remember throughout the shoot to be firm, to accept suggestions, but make your own decisions without crew pressure. Encourage your crew at all times, speaking courteously to them, even during those times when they are not doing everything the way you would like.

INTERVIEWING THE TALENT

An important element in making your own home programming is the personal interview. It is the one type of sequence that gives a program depth and a feeling of intimacy. Interviews are used very often in TV as a reliable way of informing people and discovering points of view from real sources. Your viewers are already preconditioned, from watching TV at home, to accept the interview situation as normal and natural. The types of interviews that you will be doing are one-person interviews and multiple person interviews. They can include question and answer sessions with informal group discussions or one-to-one interviews by an interviewer that may be a member of your crew.

Very often talent at each location require "warming up." Generally speaking, however, before you actually start taping, have the interviewer talk to the talent, try to relax them and get them thinking about the subjects they are going to be talking about. Rehearse talent movement if necessary. Rehearsing full answers should not be necessary. However, with confused or frightened talent, run through the major subjects to be covered in greater detail. There may be some cases where a planned interview with a special family member is very important to you. In such a case, that family member may be given the sheet titled "Tips for Facing the Video Camera" to review prior to the event (see page 115).

Once the interview begins, the responsibility of a good interviewer is to make the talent feel comfortable and make their experience of giving information a satisfying one. The interviewer should ask questions effectively, and be courteous even if he/she disagrees with the talent's point of view. The idea is not to cross-examine the people at the event; they are probably already nervous.

Start by asking talent questions that can easily be answered. Ease them into the interview. As the interview continues, do not hesitate to probe. Be assertive! This means asking questions several different ways. Some good interviewers phrase questions as many as five ways until they get the response they want. As the director, make sure the questions are known in advance and consider transitional questions to move into different areas. Be careful of the type of questions that the subject can answer with a yes or no. If a question gets answered yes/no, always follow up with a "Why?"

Use a good interview mike with a cardioid or heart-shape pickup pattern for interviewing subjects on location. This type of mike helps to eliminate unwanted noise. Always hold the microphone 6 to 12 inches from the top of the mouth. Remember that the mike is not to be used as an offensive weapon. Do not "stick" it in the subject's face; it will be intimidating. Make sure that the interviewer and the person being interviewed speaks past the top of the mike, not directly into it, which will distort the sound. The interviewer should work the mike back and forth as different subjects speak. Holding the mike stationary will not give the voice quality needed, and in some cases will result in a noticeable loss of audio. Avoid overhandling the mike. Hold it firmly. Absentmindedly rubbing and tapping the mike barrel introduces extraneous and distracting noises that are recorded on tape.

The mike should always be held in the hand of the interviewer closest to the lens of the camera, which gives the interviewer control over the interview situation. This position will also help to turn the person being interviewed and the interviewer toward the camera. If necessary, the interviewer can even take the person by the arm and gently turn him, facing toward the camera. If the subject(s) still does not have eye contact with the camera or is looking down, the interviewer can simply raise the mike, and the head of the subject(s) being interviewed will automatically rise.

When doing group interviews do not release the microphone. Once you let go, and give it to someone else in the audience, you may not get it back. The interviewer must hold the mike, and that way control the interview session, and be able to move through a variety of people. Remember, if you don't have editing equipment and you're editing in-camera as you go, you don't want to spend 45 minutes doing run-on interviews, especially if in your final program you only want to end up with 10 minutes.

COVERING THE SEQUENCES

As you follow your script, directing your crew and talent through each sequence, there will be many portions of the event where you will be using more of a documentation (observation) style of coverage. During these times you will be moving in and out of areas with your camera, working a crowd in a room, and capturing the action. You may even decide to cover an unplanned sequence as some spontaneous action suddenly "breaks" at the location. It is not unusual in action situations to stay wide-angle or zoomed out, and physically move with the camera. Less picture shake is apparent on a wide-angle shot than if you are positioned further away from the subjects and zoomed in. It is also easier to hold your focus on a wide-angle shot, especially during action, because you have greater area for the subject to move and still be in focus.

If you are not using postproduction editing, as you cover each sequence you'll want to shoot in order, so that you can edit in-camera and have an ordered playback during the viewing session. Again, we suggest you remember to hook up your recorder to a television set or a monitor. In this way, throughout the shoot you will have an instant checkpoint for the quality of your visuals and your sound. Any problems with lighting (such as hot spots), loss of focus, improper composition, or bad audio will be apparent immediately. Through the use of the TV or camera viewfinder, you can also review each sequence after you have finished shooting it. Do not move on until you have what you want. And, most of all, keep your sense of humor and your perspective. As you continue to shoot and hopefully direct off a TV set, you will develop a sense of how things should look, and a good ability to compose properly for the television screen.

As you evaluate your shots on the TV screen, remember, it is important to leave the proper amount of headroom. If necessary, allow more room for the chin and sacrifice the forehead. Also, allow for proper lead space on profiles. Giving more room in the direction the person is looking will balance the shot. Avoid poor juxtapositioning of subjects and background, and watch out for the appearance of flagpoles or plants growing out of a person's head. Also, avoid unsuitable camera-to-talent angles. Shooting down on a subject lessens the subject's authority. Shooting up on a subject increases the subject's strength and dominance. Close-up shots are powerful and emphasize what's being said. Wide-angle shots are perfect for revealing an action.

One last reminder: as you move through the taping, it is your job as the director to make people want to cooperate and to put them at ease. But that does not mean that you should be pressured into showing unprepared footage. Move through your shoot, get what you need, smile, thank everybody, and leave. Do not be discouraged by members of the audience who refuse to participate, are frightened, reluctant, or objectionable. You can ignore them, talk to them encouragingly, or try to get members who want to participate to persuade them into cooperating or leaving. As the director, do not let these people interrupt the event. Go on with your shooting, interacting positively with the members of the event who are willing to participate.

Each taping situation is challenging, exciting, and fun. From each shoot you will learn something that will make the next taping easier and more professional-looking. And, once the tape is rolling . . . enjoy . . . for you are creating a program, a "slice of real life," that you, your family, and friends will view with pleasure, time and time again.

TIPS FOR FACING THE VIDEO CAMERA (TALENT)

Content

* As you think about what you are going to say, remember, in actual presentation--the delivery usually goes slightly faster than during rehearsal.

* It is better to talk about a few ideas in a more detailed fashion, than to try to cover too many ideas which can only be touched upon lightly, due to time limitations.

* If you have a lot to say, make a brief topical outline on an index card. Go over it with the director. Do not write paragraphs. Do not confine yourself to a script, but feel free to talk naturally.

Eye Contact

* Use the "magic" of video and create that one-to-one relationship (the illusion of intimacy between you and the viewer) with eye contact. Remember, the camera is your audience. Use the lens as your reference point to reach them. Practice looking at the lens. Look at the lens as you would a person you were talking to. Look directly at the lens to add visual impact to something important you say.

Clothes

* Do not wear pinstripes, plaids, or herringbones, as they can be detrimental to picture quality. Avoid shiny jewelry that reflects bright beams of light.

* Wear clothes that are in good taste and subtle rather than bold. In general, it's best to stay away from extremes-- dark or light colors. Concentrate on contrasting <u>mid-tones</u> (blues, browns, grays), especially as they relate to skin tone. <u>Moderate contrast</u> is the key.

* Do not wear white, black, or red clothing unless the director tells you to. <u>White</u> is difficult to videograph; most cameras overcompensate for white's highly reflective quality by darkening the rest of the color picture. <u>Black</u> is too contrasting and absorbs too much color. <u>Red</u> is also difficult and can have a similar effect; in some cases it will cause the camera to render gold skin tones.

Rehearsal

* Arrive early so there is adequate rehearsal time if the director wants it.

* Do not worry about being nervous; it's natural! If you can, take a deep breath and slowly exhale. Do it a few times.

VIII

REVIEWING THE FOOTAGE

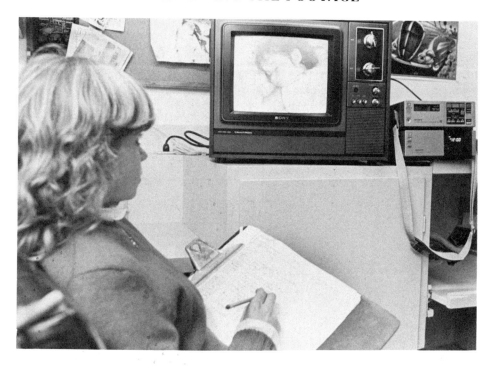

"Use the log sheet to review your footage
and note the context and visual quality of
each sequence."

CHAPTER 8

REVIEWING THE FOOTAGE

There are two places where you should review your footage: first on location, and then secondly, later at home.

LOCATION REVIEW

During the first review on location, you are still in the heat of production, rapidly checking the audio and video after each sequence before you move on to the next sequence. Being able to review your footage instantly is one of the big advantages of using videotape over film. At the location review, you have the opportunity to evaluate what you've shot, and reshoot if necessary to capture need-to-know information. Once you leave the location, the chances for re-creating the same situation if you forgot something are nonexistent.

If you choose not to check each sequence thoroughly because the event is moving too quickly, don't leave without at least spot-checking for good quality audio and video at the beginning, middle, and end of what was shot at that location. You should alert yourself to the technical quality of that sequence. If any problems did occur during that portion of the shoot, at least give yourself the option of reshooting the section later in the day, or including similar content at another location.

On location one of the major characters may want to see themselves on tape. To avoid making your talent self-conscious during additional taping, to keep from hampering the natural actions and responses of what is to follow, and to keep progressing with the shoot in a timely fashion, only show tape when the shooting is finished. While we recommend the use of a TV to review video during the production, try to keep it out of view of onlookers. This avoids people interrupting you with "helpful suggestions" and keeps you from becoming the event.

HOME REVIEW AND LOGGING

The second time you review your footage, the situation will be vastly different. It will be after the shoot has ended and in the privacy of your own home. You will be more relaxed and eager to see what you did get. This step of reviewing the footage is a time for learning. As the tape begins to play back, enjoy what you got and look for the techniques that can be used in future tapes. Do not be too critical. Do not beat yourself up for a shot missed, too shaky, out of focus, or a camera moved at the wrong time. Every shoot is a learning experience.

After you have watched the tapes through completely to get the feel of them, you are ready to start the major work of this step, which is to log the footage. To begin logging, zero the counter on the deck. Using the log sheet (provided on page 123), review your footage, analyzing and noting the quality of the content and technique of each scene. Logging is a time to become familiar with all of your footage, not to make final decisions on what to use. It's important that you write down all shots and sequences, even if you don't like them. Otherwise, at a later date, when you are going over your log to make the editing/viewing script, there just might be a sequence, interview, or shot that you eliminated that would have been perfect for your final program. By logging everything, you will have a complete record of your tape. Sometimes it's helpful to unite family, friends, or part of your crew to review the footage with you and to get their point of view.

After filling in your log sheet, you should review the tapes once again, and star those counter numbers representing sequences you would select to show in the finished program. Check the series of video sequences to see if the story line seems complete and the technique is generally acceptable. Keep in mind who your target audience is, and consider the amount of time their attention will be held by any given sequence. Generally speaking, the more personally involved the audience is with the content, the more forgiving they are of the techniques. If the content is very interesting to the audience they will overlook a loss of focus, a shaky camera, or any momentary loss of technique. For example, if the bride and groom are running down the stairs from the church to the car while rice is flying, the audience will be glad to put up with a change of focus and a camera shake in order to share the excitement of physically moving with the couple through the crowd and into the car on a wide-angle camera shot. Video gives you that very opportunity to show things as they are happening, naturally and spontaneously. In commercial TV documentaries, such as news coverage, a certain amount of technique is always sacrificed in favor of capturing reality.

LOG SHEET

Program Title_____   Date_____

Master Tape #	Counter # From To	Sequence Description	Quality of Audio and/or Video

IX

BUILDING THE TAPE

"Use the viewing script to arrange your
sequences into a finished program."

CHAPTER 9

BUILDING THE TAPE

In following Home Video Production, you have progressed through the challenge of planning and the excitement of production, and now you're getting ready to put the final program together. How you arrange your tape determines the impact it will have on its viewing audience.

There are three ways to organize your finished tape. Each involves using the log sheets and arranging your shots and sequences into a finished program. This is accomplished by making a viewing script by counter number and filling out the viewing script form provided at the end of the chapter.

MANUAL PLAYBACK

The first method is the most fundamental. It involves simply playing back the tape manually by the counter numbers in the viewing script. It can best be used if you have done on-location in-camera editing, i.e., stopping and starting your camera to shoot shots and sequences of predetermined content, composition, and length. In this way manual access time between sequences is minimized. The sequences should have included items such as reaction shots, cutaways, and establishing shots, and should have been shot chronologically, following the decisions you made during storyboarding. We suggest, in making your viewing script, that it be organized in sequences rather than shots. This will save you having to continually access short pieces, which would not maintain program continuity. Chronological sequence organization allows you to quickly locate (through fast-forward or rewind) the appropriate counter number for each sequence in the order of your viewing script. Not only will the program move smoothly this way, but not having a lot of interruptions will also hold the attention of your audience.

In preparing your viewing script, remember you will probably want to show your tape to different types of audiences, which means you may have more than one viewing script for the same event. For example, Pam may show a 10-minute program about her vacation to her friends, a 20-minute program about her vacation to her family, and also make a 40-minute program about her vacation for herself.

AUTOMATIC PLAYBACK

This second method of organizing your tape is currently available as an "index code" by several manufacturers with more manufacturers to follow. It involves using your viewing script and a special hand-held remote control to first code the tape. Playback then occurs automatically using the hand-held advance control to move the tape automatically from each sequence cue point. The indexing system uses a "tab marker," which can store a number of viewing segments permanently, play them back on command automatically, or erase them and add new ones at will.

The idea of taking your taped footage and tailoring program content and length for specific audiences, through the use of multiple viewing scripts, is made even easier with automatic playback. In the future, as microprocessors become even more inexpensive and therefore commonplace, the home video producer will be able to catalog, store, and recall a tremendous amount of different tape segments automatically.

EDITED PLAYBACK

The third method requires the most effort, but looks the most professional. It involves making an edited master from your viewing script by rerecording scenes in an order you want them on a new playback tape.

Editing uses two VCRs and possibly an automated editing controller to transfer taped footage to a new tape, building the program electronically. In editing, videotapes are not physically cut. Images and sound are transferred via cable to the new blank tape (see Appendix--editing diagrams). The information can be separated into audio and video. Manipulation of these two elements is also possible and becomes a very creative process. If you want to edit your tapes at home, there are several home video editing systems available for purchase or rental. If you want to edit your tapes, and do not want to do it yourself, use a local postproduction house to make an edited master from your tape footage using your viewing scripts. Look in any video trade magazine or phone book under "Video." Any reputable dealer of video equipment can show you how this equipment works if you ask. As a home video enthusiast, what you must remember is that you are on the ground floor of an exciting, expanding home technology. We really believe, as the home market continues to develop, that editing equipment for the home will become very affordable.

FINISHING THE PROGRAM

If you haven't already shot graphics and titles, then now is the time to consider adding them to the end of your tape, or even titling the front of your tape if you have enough room to add footage before your first video sequence. This can be done with in-camera editing. If you are using the third method, editing between two machines, graphics can be placed anywhere in the program as you build the sequences on the new tape. Remember, graphics do dress up your production and are an opportunity to give dates, times, locations, introductions to new sequences, and to give credit to your crew.

There are several ways to handle audio in building your tape. Most simple home video recorders have an audio dub capability. This enables you to add narration or music to the tape where the existing recorded sound is not needed. Music usually comes from a record turntable or audio cassette deck, and is traditionally used over titles, graphics, scenery, or footage where existing audio is noisy or undesirable. Music alone, played separately or dubbed over the tape can help move the program along. You can also perform a simple voiceover narration with a simple hand microphone plugged into your recording deck, using the VCR's audio dub function.

129

When you make an audio dub, you wipe over the existing audio. So it is also possible, when the original recorded sound is not needed, to create a new sound track by combining music, narration, and audio from the event. You can record all of these together on a separate audio cassette deck and an inexpensive audio mixer. Take this new mixed sound track which you produced on an audio cassette, and using the audio dub function, transfer the new sound to your program. If it's important to have a continuous sound reproduction of an event (e.g., presentation, graduation speech, interview, wedding vows) record this information separately on an audio cassette deck at the time you are shooting, to be dubbed later.

Once you understand all the options you have during Building the Tape, this step in the HVP plan helps mold and put the finishing touches on a personal communication. It is the time you can put a tape together to suit your needs and creative whims.

VIEWING SCRIPT

Program Title _____   Date _____

Sequence #	Master Tape #	Counter # From To	Sequence Description	Audio Dub or Voiceover	Graphics Titles

X

PRESENTING THE PROGRAM

"Arrange a comfortable seating
environment, usually a semi-circle for
small group viewing."

CHAPTER 10

PRESENTING THE PROGRAM

After spending considerable time preplanning shooting and putting your program together, the moment of presentation can indeed be a gratifying one. Home presentations have a reputation of being long drawn out viewings of slides, Super 8, and photographic albums. It is possible, however, to organize your video into a presentation that is neither too lengthy nor too boring. The key in video is the end product. How long is the tape going to be? How long can the home audience really watch the tape before they begin to tire? How long before they begin to talk during the viewing? The bottom line for a good home video presentation is: a program that people will look at, and in the end, wish there was more!

VIEWING LENGTH

A primary concern is how long is too long for any given program. We suggest that each individual program last no longer than 15 minutes. One technique is to add black between program modules on the same tape. Another, is to simply stop the tape, and only show the program in 15-minute blocks. For most guests, 15 minutes of a birthday party or your grandfather talking will be quite enough.

VIEWING ENVIRONMENT

In getting ready for the presentation, you want to develop a comfortable environment; one that's set up without distractions. For television we are talking about an environment that's not pitch black; one that has ambient light. There is an expression, "tunnelvision," which refers to TV's limited viewing field. The field of view of television is 45°. The field of view of the naked eye is 180°. If you have someone come to your home, sit down in a dark living room and watch TV, you are constricting his/her field of view all the way down to 45°. They develop an instant case of tunnelvision. This type of viewing, continuing for any length of time, becomes a very tiresome experience. If you want to increase the attention span of your audience, give them some ambient light in the environment, therefore broadening their field of view. The best lighting fixtures for a tape showing are overhead fixtures or lighting that is bounced off the ceiling. Harsh light reflecting or bouncing off the TV screen will be distracting, wiping out picture detail and viewer attention.

In creating the best of all possible environments for your program presentation, arrange a comfortable seating arrangement, usually a semicircle for small groups and a triangle for larger groups. These seating arrangements ensure your audience is not on top of each other. You should put your audience in chairs that are comfortable, but not so comfortable that they will fall asleep. Provide enough room between the chairs so that people will feel comfortable, be able to have eye contact and interact with each other, but feel that their social safety distance is maintained. This is a distance of two to three feet, eye-to-eye. The seating environment is best when each member of your audience has a "great" seat.

To also ensure that all can see well, set up the room so that the furthest anyone is sitting from the TV is equal to the diagonal measurement of your TV screen converted from inches to feet. For example: if you have a 12-inch TV, then the furthest you should be back from the TV is 12 feet. The closest that any guest should sit to the TV is half the length of the diagonal measurement converted to feet. Therefore, if you have the same 12-inch TV, the closest any guest should be is 6 feet. (See page 137.)

Ideally, place the middle of the TV screen slightly higher than viewing eye level. This provides a comfortable position for the audience to view and helps to maintain their attention. Connect the audio output of the playback machine to a sound system (see Appendix). Amplified sound will increase the audio presence in the viewing area and add a wonderful, dynamic sound quality to your program presentation.

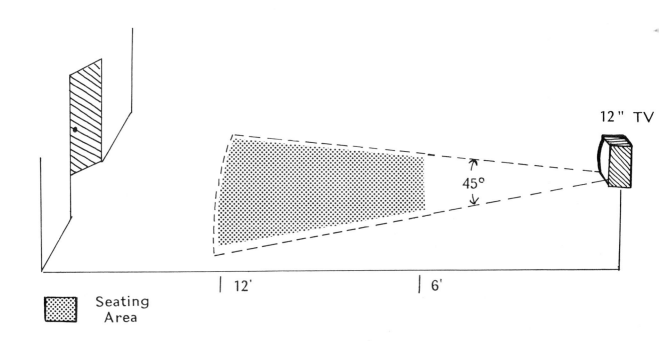

12" TV

45°

| 12'

| 6'

Seating
Area

Serve "heavy" refreshments after the showing. If you want to help them pay attention and "tune in" to your presentation, don't start a meal til after the program is over.

To maximize your chances for a good reaction from the audience, set up the environment for viewing before the guests arrive. As the host, you should introduce the program and give the context in which your shooting occurred. For example: "You're about to see our family's view of our vacation. It was the one place the whole family really wanted to go. Each one of us took turns being the cameraperson and shot the things that especially interested us."

LARGE SCREEN PROJECTORS

In trying to create a good viewing environment, many home video enthusiasts are designing home entertainment centers. The most popular type of home center is usually built around a large screen projector. The screen becomes the commanding focus of the room. It's our opinion that a most exciting way to show tape is with the use of a large screen projector. Presenting a program on a large screen projector gives a program impact and power through sheer size.

When choosing a projection system you should be sure that the room you put it in is: 1) large enough to house the unit and audience, and; 2) has a minimum of light falling on the screen. A location where the screen is away from any windows would be best. When looking at your room dimensions, think about placing the unit close to an AC outlet or think about putting an outlet in, near your unit. Exposed wires can be a real household hazard. Also, be sure to check the warranty of all the units you are interested in. Can the unit be serviced in your area? Will the service agency come to your home to work on it (since size can make it a problem to take anywhere)? Finally, the one equipment purchase that will enhance the picture on your large screen projector is a good antenna. The kind of picture your antenna picks up will be magnified on your large screen. This includes all the noise and distortions an inferior antenna picks up.

Given all the above considerations, what kind of projector to buy depends on what you can afford, and the space you have to install the unit. There are basically two types of systems. One is a single-tube system, essentially a magnification of a standard small TV. This unit is the less expensive of the two types, but does not produce the brightest picture. It requires a relatively darkened viewing space. The second kind is a 2- or 3-tube-type projector, which is more expensive but produces a brighter picture (two to four times brighter) in a normally lit room.

Large screen projectors also come in two designs: a one-piece unit that requires no focus or alignment; or a two-piece unit consisting of a screen and a separate projector which usually stands 8 to 9 feet from the screen, needs alignment, and must be in a fixed, unobstructed position. Both designs can be found in either magnified or 2- or 3-tube TV systems.

Be sure to observe and test in the showroom any unit you want, under the lighting conditions most like yours at home. You'll also want to view the picture from both left and right of center to find out how far to the sides you can view the screen before the picture becomes distorted. Both designs have built-in tuners, so you can watch broadcast TV as well as use it with your VCR. Many screen units also have additional video inputs so your screen can also be used with video games, home computer, video camera, or disc player. Manufacturers are even now packaging home video equipment, games, and accessories in component size to fit with stereo/audio equipment in wall systems.

As you produce more programming and have more viewing sessions, you may decide to join this rapidly expanding group of video people and build your own home entertainment center. It will add a whole new dimension to this final step of presenting your programs, and provide you with years of excitement as you and your audience view "larger than life" home programming in a dramatic picture and sound environment.

MAINTAINING YOUR PROGRAM LIBRARY AND SYSTEM

As you build your library of home video programs there are certain precautions you should take to extend the life of your programming and equipment.

1) Keep your recorder free from dirt. Purchase a cover.

2) At the end of every production: clean your gear, remove the batteries, and store everything in a cool, dry place. We recommend shelves. Don't stack equipment. Commercial products are available such as denatured alcohol and chamois swab, for cleaning your VCR--have your video dealer demonstrate!

3) Push in the safety tab on the back of your cassette to prevent accidental tape erasure or rerecording.

4) Store your cassettes in their cases and vertically, standing. Never store flat or on top of each other (pressure could damage tape edges).

5) Always rewind your tape to the beginning before playing. This prevents tape stretching.

6) Store your camera horizontally, never pointing lens down. Flakes from the tube will settle on tube face and leave permanent black spots which will transfer to the picture recorded.

7) Never leave equipment in the car trunk. Heat buildup can permanently damage the electronics.

8) On a regular basis (at least once a year) have your equipment professionally cleaned and checked (camera aligned, VCR tested) by a warranted service facility.

9) Avoid recording and playing back in damp areas. Machine will drag, possibly clog, damage, or even stop VCR heads.

10) Always keep lens cap on when camera is not in use. Never expose it or point it at direct sun or light source.

11) Wrap cables carefully, in a circle. Do not bend connectors.

12) Never touch your tape or the screen of a projection system. Oil from your hands will leave permanent spots.

CONCLUSION

We hope you enjoyed your first production using HVP. This program guide has stressed the importance of preplanning. The HVP approach takes all the guess work out of how your finished program will look. Each time you complete a tape using HVP, the home video experience will become easier and easier. It is a plan that will be available for you to use as a continual reference.

As you produce home programming, not only will you continue to develop an invaluable family video library, but video will become a creative vehicle for personal expression. The very act of making video will also facilitate you, your family's, and friends' ability to communicate better with each other. This new avenue of communication that arises among those of us who make and watch our own video programs, draws us closer together as pioneers in a new electronic tradition.

APPENDIX

CONNECTING YOUR VCR TO THE TELEVISION SET

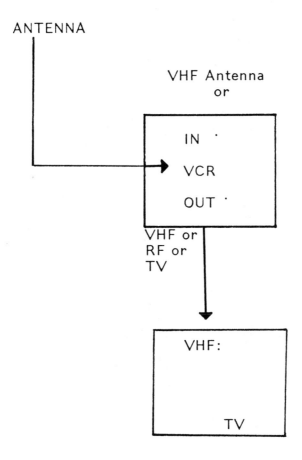

1. Disconnect antenna or cable connection from the VHF/UHF terminals on the back of your TV set.

2. Connect a cable connection directly into your VCR terminals labeled VHF or IN Antenna.

3. If you have an antenna and your connection is a twin lead 300-ohm cable,

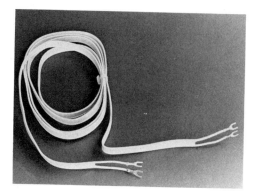

use the adaptor that comes with your VCR. It is a 300-ohm to 75-ohm connector:

You can get this adaptor at your local TV/video dealer if one does not come with your deck.

4. Connect the VHF out/RF out/TV out terminals on your VCR to the VHF terminals on the back of your TV set, using a 75-ohm coaxial cable. This cable should also come with your deck. In order to connect your TV to your VCR using the

75-ohm coaxial cable you may need a 75-ohm to 300-ohm transformer:

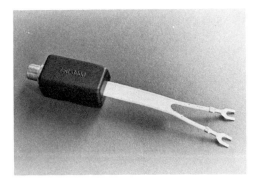

This adaptor will allow you to match up the connections on the back if necessary.

5. To receive UHF channels connect the UHF terminals on your VCR to the UHF terminals on your TV using a twin lead 300-ohm cable. If you have a combination VHF/UHF antenna, connect the coaxial or 300-ohm ribbon cable to the UHF <u>and</u> VHF IN terminals on the VCR and the output from the VCR to VHF on your TV.

6. Set your TV to either channel 3 or 4, whichever is empty in your area, when you are watching programs on your VCR. Look for a switch on the back of your VCR labeled RF converter/ch. 3 or ch. 4 and switch it to the same channel as your TV.

7. Set your tuner/timer to the correct time. If it is an external tuner/timer connect first to your VCR.

    *Remember, for regular viewing of your TV, your VCR does not have to be on but your timer switch <u>must</u> be OFF.

CABLE CONNECTIONS FOR RECORDING PROGRAMS

Fig. 1

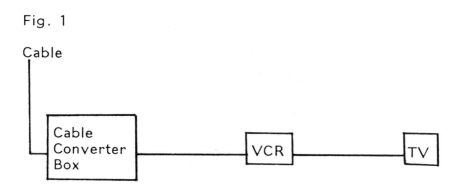

This configuration allows you to record any programs received through the converter box, whether you're watching or not. You can <u>not</u> record one program and watch another channel.

Fig. 2

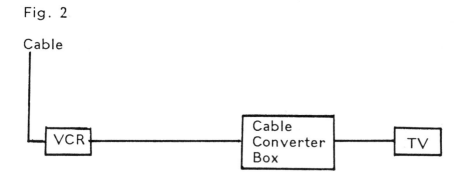

This configuration allows you to watch all the channels received through the converter box, including all special programs delivered on channels A, B, C, D, etc.

You can only record one of the twelve regular VHF channels that would regularly be delivered by cable without the converter box. This is one way to watch one program and record another.

Fig. 3

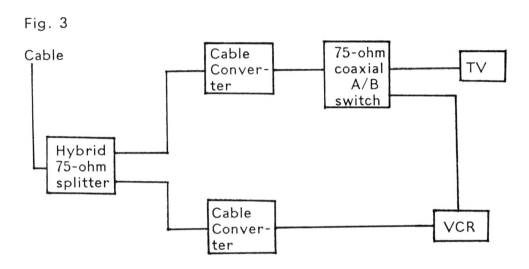

This configuration allows you to record any program your cable service supplies and watch any other program you desire. You can rent both cable converter boxes from your cable company for an additional fee. The switch and splitter can be obtained from your video dealer. If your cable company doesn't want to rent you the second converter ask your video dealer for a block converter--price around $50.

*You will not be able to program more than one event or change channels when you're away.

A long shot: You can use the second configuration and try to receive all the programming delivered by your cable without the additional converter. Set your VCR tuner select switch to 7-13 and fine tune above 13 to receive those channels your converter box receives. Don't be too disappointed if it doesn't work, but it's worth a try.

CONNECTING YOUR VCR FOR SIMULATED STEREO

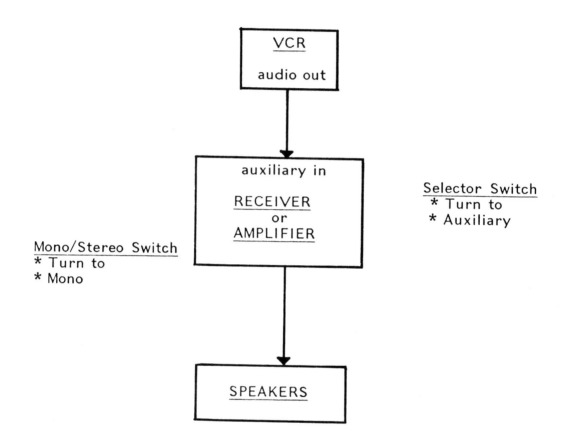

VCR

audio out

Selector Switch
* Turn to
* Auxiliary

auxiliary in

RECEIVER
or
AMPLIFIER

Mono/Stereo Switch
* Turn to
* Mono

SPEAKERS

EDITING AND DUPLICATION CONNECTIONS

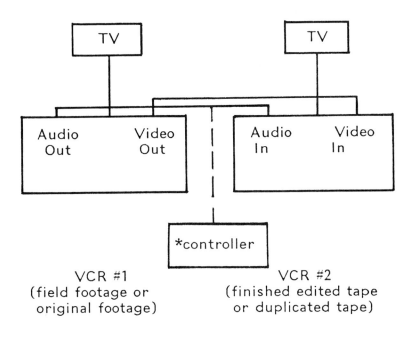

VCR #1   VCR #2
(field footage or   (finished edited tape
original footage)   or duplicated tape)

To edit segments:

1. Connect with appropriate audio cable <u>audio out</u> from VCR #1 to <u>audio in</u> at VCR #2.

2. Connect with appropriate video cable <u>video out</u> from VCR #1 to <u>video in</u> at VCR #2.

3. Connect each VCR to separate TVs. This enables you to see exactly your location on each tape, and allows you to verify duplication has occurred when you playback.

4. Cue tape on VCR #1 a few seconds before the beginning of your segment. Push "play" on VCR #1 and #2. Push "edit" button on VCR #2, a moment before the cued segment from VCR #1 appears on the TV.

5. The edit has been executed. You may see some picture disturbance at the edit point, on the tape from VCR #2.

This is to be expected and is the reason why you perform the edit before the beginning of the piece you desire duplicated.

6.   There are VCRs available that are made especially for editing and, using an "automated editing controller," they perform all these functions automatically. Contact your local home video dealer for a demonstration.

VIDEO ACCESSORIES CATALOGS

COMPREHENSIVE VIDEO SUPPLY CORPORATION
148 Veterans Drive
Northvale, NJ 07647
Attn: Mark Plitt

THE ILLUSTRATED TRADE MANUAL
The Bill Daniels Co., Markade Bldg.,
6750 West 75th Street
Post Office Box 2056
Shawnee Mission, KS 66201

WIDL VIDEO
5325 North Lincoln Avenue
Chicago, IL 60625

TOTAL VIDEO SUPPLY CORP.
9060 Claremont Mesa Boulevard
San Diego, CA 93123

GENERAL PROGRAMMING CATALOGS

Beta Videocassette Program Catalog
C.S. Tepfer Publishing Co., Inc.
Post Office Box 565, Ridgefield, CT 06877
*Entertainment, Business, Contemporary Concerns,
Documentaries, Shorts, Education, Health

Encyclopedia Britannica Educational Corp.
425 North Michigan Avenue, Chicago, IL 60611
*General Interest

Environmental Communications
64 Windward Avenue, Venice, CA 90291
*Videotape, Books, Films, Slides

Great Plains National Instructional Television Library
Post Office Box 80669, Lincoln, NE 68501
*Educational Tapes--Elementary through Adult

Public Television Library
475 L'Enfant Plaza, S.W., Washington, DC 20024
*General Interest

The Video Programs Index
The National Video Clearing House Publications
Post Office Box 3, Syosset, NY 11791
*Lists subjects and the distributors who have programming in that
category

Video Log
Essette Video, Inc.
600 Madison Avenue, New York, NY 10022
*3 volumes, General Interest/Entertainment/Business/Industry,
Health Sciences

Video Source Book
The National Video Clearing House, Inc.
Post Office Box 3, Syosset, NY 11791
*Business/Industry, Children/Fine Arts/General Interest/
Education/How To/Movies/Entertainment/Sports/Recreation

POPULAR HOME PROGRAMMING DISTRIBUTORS*

(Specialty Programming)

Magnetic Video Corporation
Industrial Park
Farmington Hills, MI 48024

Time-Life Films
1271 Avenue of the Americas
New York, NY 10020

Home Video Corp. (Rental only)
231 E. 55th Street
New York, NY 10022

VisionDisc Corp.
Post Office Box 102
Cooper Station
New York, NY 10011

Show/Tapes
886 N.E. 79th Street
Miami, FL 33138

American Educational Film
132 Lasky Drive
Beverly Hills, CA 90212

Electronic Arts Intermix
84 Fifth Avenue
New York, NY 10011

Nostalgia Merchants
6255 Sunset Blvd., Ste. 1019
Hollywood, CA 90028

Sports World, Inc.
Post Office Box 17022
Salt Lake City, UT 84117

Entertainment Unlimited Programming
848 N.W. Brooks Street
Bend, OR 97201

*Write for catalogs/information

BOOK LIST

Independent Video, by Ken Marsh, Straight Arrow Press, San Francisco, CA, 1973

The Spaghetti City Video Manual, by Video Freex, Praeger Publications, New York, NY, 1973

The Video Primer, by Richard Robinson, Quick Fox Ind., New York, NY, 1974

The Video Guide, by Charles Bensinger, Video-Information Publications, Santa Barbara, CA, 1977

The Videotape Book, by Michael Murray, Bantam Books, New York, NY, 1975

Video as a Second Language (How to Make a Video Documentary), by Don Harwood, VTR Publishing, Bayside, NY, 1975

TV Camera Operation, by Gerald Millerson, Hastings House, New York, NY, 1974

The TV Director-Interpreter, by Colby Lewis (Communications Arts Books), Hastings House, New York, NY, 1976

Eng/Field Production Handbook: Guide to Using Mini Video Equipment, by Robert C. Paulson, Broadcast Management and Engineering, New York, NY, 1976

TV Lighting Handbook, by Dr. J. A. Carroll and Dr. R. E. Shenniffs, Tab Books, Blue Ridge Summit, PA, 1977

The Writer and the Screen: On Writing for Film and Television, by Wolf Rilla, Wm. Morrow & Co., Inc., New York, NY, 1974

The Home Video Handbook, by Charles Bensinger--2nd edition, Video-Info Publications, Santa Barbara, CA, 1979

Making the Media Revolution--A Handbook for Video Tape Productions, by Peter Weiner, Available Comprehensive Catalogue, Northvale, NY, 1973

<u>Video-Cassette Recorders - The Complete Home Guide</u>, by David Lachenbruch, Everest House, New York, NY, 1979

<u>The Use of Microphones</u>, by Alex Nesbitt, Hastings House, New York, NY, 1974

<u>Television Production</u>, by Alan Wurtzel, McGraw-Hill Book Co., New York, NY, 1979

<u>The Prime Time Survey</u>, by Top Value Television, Top Value TV, Inc., San Francisco, CA, 1974

<u>Handbook for Producing Educational & Public Access Programs for Cable Television</u>, by Rudy Bretz, Educational Technology Publications, Englewood Cliffs, NJ, 1976

Note: The above list contains excellent sources of more technical information and guidance, although they may not necessarily be up-to-date in terms of the latest equipment.

VIDEO AND TELEVISION MAGAZINES

AUDIO-VISUAL COMMUNICATIONS
United Business Publications
475 Park Ave. So., New York, NY 10016

EDUCATIONAL & INDUSTRIAL TELEVISION
C.S. Tepfer Publishing Co.
607 Main Street, Ridgefield, CT 06877

HOME ELECTRONICS & ENTERTAINMENT
Harris Publications, Inc.
79 Madison Ave., New York, NY 10016

HOME VIDEO
United Business Publications
475 Park Ave. So., New York, NY 10016

TELEVISIONS MAGAZINE
Washington Community Video Center
P.O. Box 21068, Washington, DC 20009

VIDEO & HOME COMPUTERS BUYERS GUIDE
Modern Day Periodicals, Inc.
79 Madison Ave., New York, NY 10016

VIDEO MAGAZINE
Reese Publishing Co.
235 Park Ave. So., New York, NY 10003

VIDEO PLAY MAGAZINE
C.S. Tepfer Publications Co., Inc.
51 Sugar Hollow Rd., Danbury, CT 06810

VIDEO REVIEW
P.O. Box 919, Farmingdale, NY 11737

VIDEO SYSTEMS MAGAZINE
Intertec Publications Corp.
P.O. Box 12901, Overland Park, KS 66212

VIDEOGRAPHY
United Business Publications
475 Park Ave. So., New York, NY 10016